CU00690585

HR Interview Secrets

How To Ace Your Next Human Resources Interview, Dazzle Your Interviewers & LAND THE JOB YOU WANT!

Alan Collins

Success in HR Publishing
Chicago, Illinois USA

Dedicated to my son, Bryan.

Fifty percent of the proceeds of this book will
go to the Bryan A. Collins Memorial Scholarship Program
which provides scholarships to deserving, high potential
minority students who excel in academics and in
service to others. I encourage you to join me in
supporting this truly worthwhile cause at
www.BryanCollinsScholarship.org.

– CONTENTS –

HR Career Success Resources
by Alan Collins

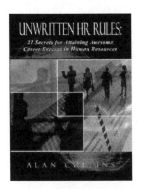

More HR Career Success Resources
By Alan Collins

YOUR HR GOLDMINE: How To Turn Your Human Resources Know-How Into A Lucrative Second Income & Make A Difference In People's Lives ... Without Leaving Your Day Job!

Available now at:
www.YourHRGoldmine.com

WINNING BIG IN HR: 100+ Powerful Strategies For Accomplishing Great Results Faster & Getting Your Clients To Rave About You As A Human Resources Professional!

Available now at:
www.WinningBigInHR.com

WRITE YOUR OWN HR BOOK FAST! Take Your HR Career To The Next Level By Authoring Your Own Book – Faster Than You Ever Thought Possible!
More Information Available at:
www.Successinhr.com/write-your-own-hr-book-fast

WHY EVEN THE BEST HR CANDIDATES NEED HELP PREPARING FOR JOB INTERVIEWS *...AND HOW THIS BOOK CAN GIVE YOU THE EDGE!*

Congratulations, you've landed an HR interview! Now, your next goal should be to dazzle your interviewers and win the job offer. And in *HR Interview Secrets* you have in your hands the best resource ever developed for enabling you to accomplish exactly that.

You'll find this book to be a tremendous resource -- regardless of your experience level. It doesn't matter if you're currently in an entry-level HR generalist or specialist, an HR manager or director, or the VP of HR responsible for setting the talent agenda for an entire organization. This book will give you the strategies and techniques you need to confidently sell yourself into your next HR job.

I know you're a busy, overworked HR pro. So this book is direct and too-the-point. And that's by design. Otherwise it would gather dust on your shelf. It has been developed to be read, digested quickly and prepare you in the fastest way possible for your upcoming interview. It contains tons of specific examples, talking points, shortcuts, case studies and time-saving tips. There's simply no other resource like it.

Will this book guarantee you an HR job? Of course not. No career coach, recruiter, training program or interview guide can do that. But what this particular book will do is guarantee that if you follow the suggested techniques and strategies:

- You will be exceedingly more confident, fully prepared and less anxious going into your interviews.
- You will have an outstanding game plan and strategy that will enable you to stand out from other HR candidates.
- You will know how to handle difficult, awkward or un-planned situations that inevitably come up in interviews.
- When the interview is over, you will feel as if you came across powerfully and you'll leave extremely proud of your performance.
- You'll know how to avoid mistakes, close the deal and negotiate a strong compensation and benefit package for yourself.

What more could you ask for?

Having said all that, let's deal upfront with a question that might be rolling around in your head at this point. And that is...

I'm In Human Resources. Why Would I Possibly Need Help Interviewing?

Great question. You may already be an absolute pro at inter-viewing. In fact, if staffing and talent acquisition is part of what you do daily, you may interview hundreds of job candidates every month.

However, there's a BIG difference when you're on the other side of the table as an interviewee. When someone else is in control of the interview and when it's *your own* career on the line, the challenge and level of difficulty is much greater. And if you haven't interviewed in awhile, you're rusty and it's easy to overlook the basics and finer points of positioning your-self as a compelling candidate.

Having spent over fifteen years of my career interviewing candidates ranging from entry-level HR reps to experienced HR

VPs, I've seen tons of well-qualified people who look great on paper flunk the interview and blow their chances at getting an offer only because they couldn't handle the subtle dynamics of selling themselves convincingly one-on-one to a group of interviewers.

If that weren't enough, there's this...

You Need An Edge Because The Competition For HR Positions At All Levels In Today's Job Market Is Fierce.

To land a job in this up and down market, history shows that you will probably need at least eight specific job opportunities before you land a job offer. This means suiting up, persisting, surviving rejection, and reaching the last round of interviews on at least eight different occasions!

And that's not all. The higher the level of the HR position you're interviewing for, the more complex the interviewing process is going to be. More people involved. Tougher questions. Multiple rounds of interviews. And the more time you can expect to devote to the interview process before a decision is made. In fact, it is not unusual to hear that some organizations require candidates speak with 15 to 25 interviewers face-to-face and go through three to five rounds of interviews before making a final decision.

This book will give you the advantage you need to successfully navigate the hidden dynamics and landmines of this process and arrive safely at the finish line with job offer in hand.

With that in mind...

Here's How To Quickly Squeeze The Most Juice From This Book

#1: Take a few minutes to speed scan through entire book. It's very detailed and thorough. Get a good sense for how the chapters are sequenced and laid out. The key points are bolded and will pop off the page with the most important ideas.

#2: Pick out and prioritize those ideas most relevant to where you are currently in the interview process. Underline or highlight those key sentences and chapters first -- and make these a part of your interview plan.

#3: Finally, customize the ideas to your own situation. Plenty of examples, talking points and case studies are provided to bring these practical ideas to life. Some of them will fit your situation. Others won't. But most can be adapted so that they can add significant value to your interview preparation. Realistically, if you use 30% of what's in this book, you'll be ahead of the game. If you use 50% or more, you'll be absolutely golden.

A WARNING: The advice in this book is not meant to encourage you to lie, misrepresent yourself or provide false and misleading information to employers. As an HR professional, your integrity is the most important attribute you can bring to your new position. And you should do nothing to compromise it.

Finally, if you've read my previous books know that I like to keep things simple and this book will be no different. You'll find the concepts described here practical and easy to put into action. Nothing is held back. This is the real deal to help you prepare to emerge as a top candidate for the position.

I wish you much success,

Alan Collins

Alan Collins

1

FIRST THINGS FIRST: CONQUER YOUR INTERVIEW FEARS, ANXIETIES & JITTERS

Everyone gets nervous before interviews.

It doesn't matter if you have twenty-years of experience in HR and have interviewed hundreds of job candidates yourself as a recruiter. When you flip over to that other side of the table as an interviewee, it can be stressful.

And there is only one way to conquer your fears, anxieties and nervousness…

<u>P</u>reparation & <u>P</u>ractice!

If you want to be perceived as a polished, sharp, ready-for-prime-time HR professional, these <u>two P's</u> must be at the top of your to-do list.

However, it's important to remember that a certain amount of anxiety in a stressful situation is good. It's healthy, normal and natural…and may actually make you sharper and help you perform better.

The problem occurs when that small amount of anxiety becomes a debilitating case of fear that forces you to stumble over your words, freeze up when facing tough questions and not come across at your best.

That's what strong practice and preparation can help alleviate. Amazingly, according to *Career Builder,* 78 percent of all candidates simply wing it in interviews. This is an unforgivable sin today, when so much helpful information is easily accessible online. Even with candidates who do prepare, few do so in the in-depth way that will distinguish them from their competition.

Your preparation and practice is no different than the way pro athletes like Serena Williams or LeBron James train to be in peak condition on the day of the big game. Or world-class singers like Taylor Swift or Tony Bennett, who practice and rehearse for hours on end before their big performances. Like them, the more you prepare and practice, the more confident you'll feel when your career aspirations are on the line in the job interview.

With all this in mind, here's a checklist of steps to follow to calm your fears:

Step #1:
Set aside at least 4 hours to study the key chapters in this book to jack up your confidence before each interview.

This is an absolute must! The specific chapters where you should focus that time are as follows:
1. **Preparing Yourself (this Chapter & Chapters 4-10)**
2. **Knowing What Employers Want To See (Chapter 2)**
3. **Knowing the Employer Like An Insider (Chapter 3)**

Why four hours?

Because that's the advice of Lou Adler, author of *Hire with Your Head*, one of America's most admired executive recruiters.

He advises his job candidates to prepare between 4-10 hours (with 4 hours being the absolute minimum).

And I agree 100%.

If you haven't interviewed in awhile, you're no doubt rusty and out of practice – and that can hurt you when show time comes. In addition, what were considered great interview behaviors and responses ten years ago could actually prevent you from a getting a job these days. The job climate has shifted and employers have different expectation for HR candidates than they did even five years ago.

Reviewing these key chapters can help you overcome all of these obstacles. In addition, they will help you with other absolutely essential preparation steps, which include:

- **Knowing your interviewers (pages 31-33).**
- **Tips for researching the employer (pages 33-34).**
- And much, much more!

Step #2:
Practice rehearsing your answers to anticipated questions to fine-tune the main messages you want to convey.

Do this as part of your 4 hours of minimum preparation. **You'll find lots of excellent questions to assist you in Chapters 5-7.** Even if you are an excellent presenter, it's crucial that you use these questions to verbalize your answers and responses.

Because speaking is a physical activity, it will improve with repetition. You can't adequately do this in your head. Having information in your brain and articulating that same information with your mouth are two very different activities.

Rehearsing what you will say in advance creates muscle memory, so you'll be able to more quickly gather your thoughts, deliver your message, and be less nervous during the actual interview. Here are some ways to make that happen:

- **Practice looking in the mirror and answering questions out loud.** This prep work will help you clarify your thoughts and make you much more comfortable during the interview. It will also help you address any mannerisms you may need to correct. For example, you may use too many informal words like "totally" and "awesome" or speak way too quickly which can undermine your message and hinder your chances of getting hired.

- **Set up as many mock interviews and role play sessions as you possibly can with a trusted friend or colleague.** Or practice in front of your smartphone – and audio or video record these sessions. When playing them back, turn off the sound at some point and just pay attention to your facial movements, posture, and mannerisms to get a feel for how your body language comes across.

- **Don't be afraid to stumble over answers to questions like *"Tell me about yourself?"* or *"Why should we hire you?"*** Do this a number of times until your responses feel meaty, succinct, and comfortable. Then, infuse your voice with energy and optimism. You'll be much better at answering these kinds of questions the twentieth time you've done it versus your first time. Guaranteed.

Step #3:
Practice staying positive.

Mentally resolve that you won't whine, blame, criticize, or complain about former managers or previous employers.

Interviewers bypass negative candidates. They worry that such candidates will poison their work environment, exasperate their colleagues and will prove difficult to work with. So avoid negativity at all costs.

To help you in this area, ask yourself the following as you practice responding to mock interview questions:
- How might this be worded in a more positive light?
- Is what I'm saying building or destroying my case?
- Is my response making the interviewer more confident and certain I can do the job?

Never act discouraged or display your frustrations, even if you sense that the interview isn't going well. Violating this rule will only sink your candidacy faster than you can say

Step #4:
Plan to avoid talking for
more than 2 minutes straight.

When rehearsing your responses, make sure you time them – and avoid memorizing answers word for word. Instead, jot down and review a few key words for each answer and practice them until these responses come naturally. A response lasting one to two minutes, or a little longer if you're answering a behavioral interview question (Chapter 6) is fine. However, if you need to talk longer, break up the response with a question midway, such as one of these:

- *"Am I giving you the details you need?"*
- *"Would you like an example of that?"*
- *"What have you seen to be the case in your organization?"*

Step #5:
Watch your pauses.

Your ability to quickly recall the details from the work experiences on your resume affects whether you'll be invited back and if you'll get an offer.

Years ago, I recently watched a HR VP candidate crash and burn during an interview. While her answers were perfect and naturally delivered, she paused for three or four seconds before answering each question. In an interview, that's a lifetime.

For every moment an employer sees you think, you lose credibility. You need to be prepared to speak within one short breath after the other person stops talking. This conveys confidence and preparation.

Step #6:
Lay out your interview attire ahead of time.

Your visuals make a statement about you before you even open your mouth. Even in today's increasingly casual work environment, a scuffed shoe, a messy bag, or a low cut blouse can speak volumes. So you should plan to get your personal appearance right in advance. **Half the battle in coming across confidently is proving that you belong and can be part of the team.**

In his terrific book, *Work Rules!*, Laszlo Bock shares his experience being recruited as the global head of People Operations at Google -- their top HR job. After three years at GE, he was ready to make a job change.

He remembers the recruiter, Martha Josephson, trying to convince him not to wear a suit to the interview. "No one wears suits there," she assured him, "and they'll think you don't understand their culture if you show up in one." He took her advice and dressed "business casual" with just a jacket, collared shirt and slacks and got the job. But he was also skeptical enough that as insurance he carried a necktie stuffed into his jacket pocket in case he needed it.

The point: Wrong choices in attire can show poor judgment and that you didn't do your homework on the basics of how to best fit into the employer's workplace. HR executives, in particular, are accustomed to making quick judgments about people. So even if you're a phenomenal candidate, showing up in the wrong attire can be the kiss of death. You may only get one shot, so you need to make it count. Here are some **guidelines on what to wear to make a positive first impression:**

Conduct a little research. Are you interviewing with a company where the leaders and employees still wear dressy shirts, ties, skirts and heels every day; or does everyone dress in a more relaxed and business casual fashion; or do t-shirts and jeans prevail? Do yourself a favor and nail this ahead of time.

How?

Call the recruiter, hiring manager or a friend that works at the company and ask them what is recommended as far as dress code is concerned. Or check out photos of management and employees on the company's website. Or you could even scout the office and see what attire employees favor. If you know anyone at the company you're interviewing with, ask them about the environment and culture. Hang out a coffee shop across the street and get a glimpse at what people are wearing.

Once you've done this, then dress ONE STEP ABOVE the normal work attire of the company. If you're a guy and the normal work attire of the company is "business casual" (jacket and/or open collared shirt), then wear a suit and tie. If the work attire is casual and predominantly jeans (like what Laszlo Bock encountered at Google), then dress "business casual" (open collared shirt, slacks and carry your jacket). If no dress code is mentioned, wear a jacket and tie anyway just to be on the safe side (you can then just take your jacket off and stuff your necktie into your jacket pocket, if the situation dictates). If you are wearing a suit, you can't go wrong in a navy blue or dark gray color, white or light blue shirt and a conservative, low-key tie.

If you're a woman, wearing a jacket, skirt and heels (instead of pants and flat shoes) allows you to come across as more professional and experienced. With your jacket, you can be flexible. You can throw it on to formalize and leave it off to be more casual. Don't overdo the makeup and lipstick. Avoid skirts that are too short or tight, low-cut blouses that show too much cleavage, extremely high-spiked stiletto shoes or excessive perfume or makeup. Anything you wear should be crisp which means no wrinkles, stains, lint, holes, or snags.

And for anyone, _unless you're told otherwise,_ absolutely avoid jeans or yoga pants for any of your very <u>first</u> HR interviews...even if the environment is stunningly relaxed and casual ...and the people you're talking with are currently wearing them at work. _They already have their job -- you don't yet!_

Finally, carry and wear the brand – not the competition's! This is crucial. If you're interviewing at Armani, do not wear Tommy Hilfiger. If you're at PepsiCo, do not come in carrying a

Coke in your hand. If you do, and you're a seasoned HR pro, your judgment will be questioned. Some interviewers are unforgiving on these tiny oversights.

Step #7:
Pack essential items ahead of time to minimize last-minute scrambles.

The night before, besides your attire, pack everything else you think you might need. Use this checklist to spark your own ideas about what to bring to the interview:

- **Resume.** Bring at least 10 copies. You may need to hand them out to others you meet, and it's easier if you have them with you rather than the interviewer potentially scrambling at the last minute to make copies – or wasting your time attempting to retrieve them if they've been misplaced. Being prepared in this way also demonstrates your ability to plan ahead, and further shows your genuine interest in the position.
- **Cover letter** if you sent one originally. In case any questions come up, it's helpful to have a copy.
- **Position description/job posting,** if applicable.
- **List of questions you wish to ask your interviewers.** These should be written out and in your portfolio or on your smart phone. See Chapters 8 and 9 for examples.
- **Business cards.** If you don't have business cards from your current job, or prefer not to hand them out during your job search, have some professionally printed or use one of the many easy-to-use computer programs to create your own.
- **Two nice pens and a note pad.**
- **Specific requests the interviewer may have made,** such as performance reviews, references, school transcripts, and the like. Make sure your references know in advance that the potential employer might contact them.

- **Single briefcase, laptop bag or a neat leather portfolio/folder** to accommodate your key documents. It presents a more polished image if you have your materials neatly organized in one place instead of multiple tote bags, handbags, or no bag at all. Be sure that your case includes only materials relevant for the interview at hand. (Under the pressure of an interview, it's too easy to quickly grab and pull out a document that you're certain is your reference sheet, for example, only to have it turn out to be a handout from a previous interview.)
- **Cell phone** (be sure to turn it off when you arrive!).
- **Your credit card and a few dollars of extra cash** (small bills and loose change can work quickly for cab fare, parking meters, parking garages and restaurant tips).
- **Lip balm, facial tissues, small comb and/or brush** for last-minute primping.
- **Small mirror** in case one isn't readily available in the restroom (it happens!).
- **Breath mints** or dissolving breath-freshening sheets.
- **Flash Drive.** Bring a flash drive with all your key documents in case your employer asks for a hard copy of a document for which you do not have a printed version. This way you will save time and demonstrate your efficiency and organization.
- **Driver's License.** For corporate security purposes, many employers require visitors to show identification and still others will make a copy of your ID before clearing you for entry onto their premises. It may also be requested to validate information for a background check.
- **An up-to-date calendar.** In case they want to schedule another interview on the spot!

Finally, you want to present as uncluttered and streamlined a picture as possible. And that's hard to do when you're loaded down with things like paperback novels, shopping bags, fast food and umbrellas (unless it's raining). Leave all these kinds of distracting, non-essential items at home. Carry as little as possible with you, and make the best impression you can.

Step #8:
Do a drive by or a site visit in advance to ensure you don't arrive late.

Tardiness shows disrespect, poor planning and horrible judgment on your part. But it happens more frequently than it should, especially in large cities with frequent traffic snarls.

As part of your prep, it's a good idea to take a quick drive-by to where your interview will take place or visit the actual site the day before your meetings. This can ensure that you don't get lost on the way. Google maps is not always reliable and doing this in advance can give you an opportunity to check out the parking situation.

Even if you know exactly where you're going, make sure to give yourself plenty of time to get there on the day of and ask for the interviewer's direct phone number – accidents or traffic tie-ups do happen. So call or text if something occurs or there is far more traffic than you anticipate, and you're going not going arrive on time.

Plan to get to the location 15-30 minutes before the meeting. Arriving sooner than this is a waste of time and such displays of eagerness are unnecessary. While you're waiting, review your resume or the job description again or do a few of the quick mental preparation exercises in Step #9 that follows.

Step #9:
Do visual imagery exercises for 5-10 minutes a few times before your interview to reduce your anxiety.

Visualizing success is the secret technique just about all world-class athletes use before their competitions to improve

their performance. When done correctly, you are getting your brain ready to behave in the way that you desire.

Here's how it works:

Find a quiet space where you won't be disturbed, close your eyes and visualize yourself being successful in your interview. Picture the ideal outcome of the interview. See yourself relaxed, comfortable and engaged -- responding well to the "Why have you had so many jobs?" question or other tough questions that you might be concerned about.

Notice the employer's smile and head-nods as he or she listens to you sharing your experience.

Picture yourself demonstrating to the employer how you would do the job or handle a particular HR situation. Listen to yourself wrapping up the interview with a closing that nails the most important aspects of your candidacy.

Visualize the interviewer saying, "You are just what we've been looking for," or, if it's a second or third interview, "We'd like you to come on board."

Don't scoff at these mental preparation techniques or un-derestimate their power. They will get you in the right frame of mind and strengthen your self-assurance.

It's important that you keep reminding yourself over and over that you are well-qualified and bring significant potential value to the employer or you wouldn't have been invited to the interview in the first place. If you don't honestly believe this, there is no way that you be will able to convince the interviewer that you are the best person for the job.

If you need additional help here, review your resume and your list of HR key initiatives you've worked on and accomplishments you've had. You can even visualize those past situations where you were most successful. Once you remind yourself of your abilities in these areas, you will feel stronger.

Keep in mind that the interview is nothing more than a business meeting. If you've been in HR for any length of time, you have tons of experience in participating and leading business gatherings. When your HR colleagues, clients, or managers need something from you, you figure out how to deliver it…and that typically requires a series of business meetings to make it happen. The interview is no different. Your potential employer needs something from you. The interview is your opportunity to show them that you can deliver it.

So, enjoy the interview and be proud of your achievements. Remember to slow down, listen and be yourself. If you do that, you'll come across as relaxed, authentic and confident.

Summary

Nervousness is natural before interviews. However, following the nine steps in this chapter allows you to be well-prepared and gives you an immediate advantage over other HR candidates. In addition, being well-rehearsed will take the edge off of your pre-interview anxiety.

Experts say the number one key to making money in real estate is *location, location, location.* Well, I say the number one key to winning interviews and getting the salary you deserve is:

PREPARATION, PREPARATION, PREPARATION
and
PRACTICE, PRACTICE, PRACTICE!

2

KNOW WHAT EMPLOYERS ARE LOOKING FOR IN TOP HR CANDIDATES

If you've ever blown an interview, you know it's next to impossible to get truly accurate and detailed feedback afterwards. The hiring manager is either too busy, not interested or doesn't want the hassle of debating with you or saying the wrong thing.

Instead, you'll get closed out with a standard rejection note or phone call. It shouldn't be that way. But unfortunately that's life in most large organizations.

So, in lieu of getting direct feedback from them, this chapter lays out the **ten key qualities** that most savvy interviewers are looking for in HR candidates -- irrespective of the position for which you're interviewing.

As part of your interview prep, it's important that you know what these are so that you can seize every opportunity showcase them in your interviews. They include your:

1. **HR Functional Knowledge**
2. **Leadership Capability**
3. **Business Acumen**
4. **Promotions and Career Moves**
5. **Track Record of Results**

6. **Critical and Unique Experiences**
7. **Cultural "Fit"**
8. **Energy and Enthusiasm**
9. **Communications Skills**
10. **Ability to Meet The Job's Demands**

The more of these qualities you have, the greater the chance that you'll positively differentiate yourself from the rest of the pack.

Let's take each one of these one by one:

#1: Your HR Functional Knowledge

Interviewers will first and foremost be looking to see if you know your stuff in your HR area of expertise. For example, if your specialty is compensation, they'll be looking for you to demonstrate a strong command of hourly, salaried and executive pay approaches, incentive and bonus best practices and well as the emerging trends in the field.

Likewise, if you're interviewing for an HR generalist role, you'll need to wow them with your ability to be a jack-of-all-trades and juggle a wide variety of talent, employee and work-place issues and dilemmas with poise.

However, once you reach an executive or the VP level, functional knowledge in HR is assumed. And the emphasis then shifts to other areas such as your critical experiences or your leadership capability.

Speaking of which, let's tackle...

#2: Your Leadership Capability

Obviously, leadership increases in importance as you interview for more senior HR roles.

But frankly, no matter what level of an organization your HR role lies, employers want to know that you bring with you the ability to lead, influence, sell your ideas and effectively resolve issues with your clients, colleagues and employees -- whether they report directly to you or not.

HR folks with proven skills in taking charge and getting others to follow them are always in demand. It doesn't matter if you were never formally appointed as the head of a department or given a leadership title.

So, if you've had success leading others on projects, task forces or teams, many employers will consider this one of the biggest assets you bring to the party.

#3: Your Business Acumen

Interviewers will want to know that you not only understand the tactical needs of HR, but that you also understand their business as well. The best companies expect HR people to be passionate about their products and services and not shy away from participating in business-related discussions.

In fact, the true superstars in HR are business people first and HR people second. They can hold their own talking about the business with just about any business leader on their team. In fact, if the general manager was out sick, many of them could step in and give a 15-minute monthly business update to the leadership team, if needed.

Doing your research on the company as described in Chapter 3 will be crucial to enabling you to demonstrate your knowledge of their organization and your business acumen.

In fact, my favorite piece of HR advice is:

"It's easy to impress your business leaders as an HR professional -- when you've impressed them with your knowledge of their business first!"

#4: Your Promotions & Career Moves

Interviewers assume that the strongest HR candidates get promoted more rapidly. They either get assigned to bigger roles or progress rapidly by heading up important projects or key initiatives. Because of this, they'll focus on the last 5-10 years of your career to see if the following have been trending upward:

- your job titles
- the number of employees you've supported
- your dollar budget accountability
- your number of direct reports
- and the overall scope and impact of your assignments.

They'll be looking to see if there is an advancing pattern to your work history. The hiring manager, in particular, will be probing deeply to determine what you've done that enabled you to move to these new assignments. He or she will be trying to figure out was it because of luck or seniority...or, better yet your strong HR functional skills or dynamic team and leadership capabilities.

Self-initiated job changes can be revealing also. They'll want to understand why and how you went from one organization to another -- and the overall comparability of the companies and industries you've worked in. That will provide a rough idea if you're progressing appropriately in your career.

Many people leave job for superficial reasons and accept offers without conducting the appropriate due diligence. Lack of progression is a clue this is the case. Most interviewers assume the best HR people primarily leave jobs for lack of career opportunities and then get better opportunities as a result.

With that in mind, another obvious attribute of yours that will be examined closely is...

#5: Your Track Record of Results

Organizations prefer to hire HR pros with a proven track record of high achievement. These are folks who go beyond the call of duty to deliver better-than-expected results. Interviewers will be looking for cues that demonstrate this in your interview.

So, being able to <u>quantify</u> or <u>dollarize</u> your successes and accomplishments is a winning formula as you pitch your qualifications...no matter how much or how little HR experience you've had.

For example, if you've *"Helped cut Brand Manager talent acquisition costs by $175,000 through improvements in using social media to attract candidates"* or if you've *"Improved the employee retention rate from 85% to 96% in the customer service group,"* expect these kinds of contributions open eyes and grab attention, especially if the employer is facing similar issues.

Closely related to your track record is...

#6: Your Critical or Unique Experiences

Not all HR assignments are created equal. The HR challenges can be dramatically different if you're working in a rapid-growth environment (Apple)...versus a fix-it, business turnaround situation (General Motors, Ford)...versus a mature non-for-profit organization (United Way).

However, all of these challenges provide unique HR experiences that can be in extremely high demand by a specific employer. So, it's crucial that you define the types of experiences you've had so you can position them to your advantage in your discussions.

Also as more organizations globalize, any HR-related experience outside of the U.S. can be a differentiator. If you speak a foreign language, that's a big plus too. Even if you've haven't done any of these things, showing evidence that you studied abroad, completed a foreign exchange program or worked successful with businesses in other countries (e.g. Brazil, Russia, India, China, etc), can be a competitive edge for you with organizations with locations spread around the world.

Then there's...

#7: Your "Cultural Fit"

Many outstanding HR candidates get dropped from the interview process because they don't "fit" the culture.

Cultural fit relates to your personal ability to mesh with the company's environment, pace, intensity, personality and its values and mission.

For example, if there's a need to work with a bunch of aggressive, me-first personalities who are difficult to deal with, this becomes part of what's being sought by the interviewer.

Likewise, if the pace of the company is very demanding, lacks adequate resources or has unclear expectations...your ability to thrive and not freak out in this type of culture will be weighed heavily in the mind of your interviewers.

Many organizations have hired talented HR people who got frustrated and failed because they couldn't adapt to the organization's pace (either too fast or too slow), their unstructured environment, or a vague or less defined HR role.

Hiring cultural misfits is a common and serious problem that employers want to avoid. And so do you.

#8: Your Energy & Enthusiasm

Nobody wants to hire a whiner. Negative energy is a turnoff and despite your best efforts to conceal it, it can creep into your interview. Especially if you're stepping into your meetings angry at having been looking for a job for so long that you've become frustrated with the whole job search process.

Sure, if you were fired, laid off or forced out of your last organization unjustifiably, you have every right to be bitter. However, bringing this with you into your interview sessions and dropping little subtle digs at your former boss or company will cost you. Even if it feels good to verbally vent to someone, the interview isn't the time and place.

I'm sure this is obvious and you know all this already, but it's important to check yourself!

Surveys of hiring managers and HR leaders show that the one of the top qualities they seek are non-jaded, HR folks who are positive and inspiring. Your passion, positive energy and enthusiasm for the job sells and will hide many of your other shortcomings as an HR pro. Interviewers and most HR folks want to be around other people who are upbeat, exciting and at the very least, positive.

So wherever it comes from, fight negative energy. It's a distraction that will sap the positive elements of your presentation and seriously damage whatever chances you have of making a great impression.

It may be tough, but find something positive to say about an organization or boss that laid you off without warning – even if you must dig deep to find it. Think about something that you learned from your old boss or accomplished with his or her help. Think about all the skills that you learned and all the ways that you grew your career during your tenure at your last employer. Think of all the things you are grateful for. This type of positive attitude will go a long way in your interviews.

#9: Your Communications Skills

The worst HR director candidate I ever interviewed was boring as hell. The way he communicated nearly put me to sleep during our session. He spoke in a robotic, monotone voice with no enthusiasm whatsoever. I sat there trying hard to stay awake and listen as he talked me step-by-step through every single freaking job and work assignment he had over the past ten years.

While he had an impressive resume, his accomplishments just got buried in the irrelevant details he felt compelled to talk about. As a result, he didn't engage or keep me interested. Had he been more selective in what he communicated and injected more passion into his voice in relating his experiences, it probably would have made more of an impact. Sadly, he came across the same way to the other interviewers and was dropped quickly from the selection process.

Right or wrong, the perception of interviewers is that HR people who communicate well are on the ball and exude confidence. And that the less effective communicators lack a sense of urgency, appear unmotivated and are a drag to be around. Whether this is true or not doesn't matter. What matters is that you address this perception.

What do you do? First of all, do your own personal gut check to determine how you come across. Get some honest feedback from a trusted colleague about how you sound. Do an autopsy of your interviews and networking exchanges. Do you come across in person as someone who is blah, boring, flat, overly-detailed, disengaged and lethargic?

Once you've done this assessment, determine how you might inject more interest, drive and enthusiasm into your voice and how you come across. Most interviewers, clients and HR folks want to be around other people who effective and engaging communicators.

And that brings us to…

#10: Your Ability To Meet The Job's <u>Immediate</u> Demands & Needs

I've saved this for last because it's the most important factor. You can have all nine of the other qualities, and have terrific long-term potential…but if your specific talents don't fit the immediate demands for the job, you can get passed over.

Most employers want HR candidates who can hit the ground running as quickly as possible – preferable on day one. So it's critical that you have a deep familiarity with the position's <u>immediate requirements and needs</u> so that you can position yourself as the ideal candidate they're lusting after, right NOW!

To do this requires that you:

Define The HR Role Itself: What are its key accountabilities? Who does the position report to? Who are the key clients that will be serviced by this role? How will success be measured? What the prior incumbent in the job did well (or not so well)?

Define The Major HR Priorities: In which areas are they looking specifically for you to add immediate value? What are the biggest pain points and challenges facing the role? For example, is the job's big challenge:
- Improving the retention of top engineering talent?
- Handling tough employee relations issues?

- Improving engagement and work group morale?
- Developing a brand new HR strategy?
- Leading/participating in a major HR change initiative?
- Helping to restructure the workforce to reduce overhead?
- Attracting higher quality job candidates in R&D?
- Raising the performance of their customer service reps?
- Improving the results from the sales force?
- Addressing the lack of a talent pipeline in some regions?
- Changing the skill mix of the front-line workforce?
- Creating a positive labor climate and staying non-union?
- Relocating jobs to lower cost areas of the country?
- Improving teamwork between two functions at war?
- Spreading best HR practices internally?
- Reducing overtime, tardiness or sick leave usage?

It could also be any one, combination of the above or something different entirely. But it's essential that you pin this down!

Let's say based on your assessment, they are looking for an experienced HR generalist with the ability to lead project teams, influence clients and sell their ideas. Here are some examples of accomplishments you could speak to in the interview that illustrate your abilities in this area:

- *I proactively led the development of a new attendance policy which reduced absenteeism levels at our Chicago location by 2% year-on-year*
- *I suggested the adoption of three new innovative HR approaches which improved employee engagement, two of which were immediately adopted. And all of them together led to a 23% improvement in our Dallas plant survey results.*
- *I assembled and led a cross-functional team which expanded the scope of HR services provided by 25%. To do this, required that I work with the team to overcome resource limitations, conflicts, communication breakdowns and gaining approval from the company's Executive Committee.*

Here's a different example, let's say the organization's is coming off of a tough year and their biggest priority is simply reducing costs. You could highlight your previous experience in:

- *Developing non-monetary incentive or recognition programs for employees who help drive down costs.*
- *Using referral programs to attract talent that allows managers to hire dedicated, but less expensive employees for lower skilled positions.*
- *Providing advice and tools for reducing unnecessary overtime at manufacturing locations.*

It is this ability to know what the employer's <u>real needs are</u> and <u>how you can help address them RIGHT NOW</u> is what will impress your interviewers, differentiate you from others and make you a top candidate.

How To Get The Information Needed To Position Yourself As A Compelling HR Candidate

Ask for a Position Profile or Job Description. This is the obvious first step to take before the interview. If the company can't give you one, be wary. This is a potential red flag that the employer isn't yet clear on the job and that it may take awhile for them to fill it while they decide what they're looking for. Ask the recruiter or the HR representative who set up your interview to e-mail the position description to you.

Contact the Hiring Manager. As part of your preparation for your interview, contact the hiring manager. This seems like a ridiculous idea to many candidates; after all, the hiring manager is crazy busy, has no time to spend talking with you about an upcoming interview, and will only be annoyed at you for being pushy. Let me ask you – what is a greater priority for the hiring manager than hiring the best qualified person? Shouldn't she take time to help you and other candidates present your best in the interview?

I suggest the following strategy: Email the hiring manager and request 15 to 20 minutes of her time to ask questions about the basic job requirements. During the call, have a list of five to seven questions you want to ask. Make sure the questions will provide information you need to develop your interview presentation, and maintain a strict 20-minute time limit. See a list of potential questions in Chapter 8.

Admittedly, this strategy is rife with obstacles. There may be an admin or an internal recruiter who is running interference for the hiring manager. The hiring manager might want to avoid any contact with a candidate that could influence the hiring decision. And biggest downside of all, it's just not how it's usually done. Having had a number of my HR colleagues follow this strategy, I can report the following:

- Some were successful, having a very productive 20-minute conversation.
- Even when there wasn't a conversation, several hiring managers were impressed by my colleagues' attempts to be well prepared for their interviews.
- Not one colleague reported any negative consequences of reaching out to the hiring manager.

The key is to gather as much data as you can before the meeting so you will know as much as you can.

Summary

These are the **ten crucial qualities** to keep in mind as you prep. You'll want to take advantage of every opportunity to clearly communicate and demonstrate these attributes to your interviewers – especially #10.

3

KNOW THE EMPLOYER
LIKE AN INSIDER

As mentioned previously, employers are impressed with HR candidates who display deep insights into and a passion for their business. This gives them a strong reason to believe that you'll be excited about working there and committed to their success.

To pull this off successfully requires doing your homework in advance. Your goal should be to become as familiar with their organization as any current manager or insider would, even though you don't work there yet.

This may sound daunting, but it isn't. It requires taking some time to research and strengthen your knowledge of:

1. The Employer's Business
2. Their Strategy
3. Their Culture
4. Your Interviewers

Here's a breakdown of each of these areas, starting with…

Knowing The Employer's Business

This means diving into the details of the business. For example, for an interview at PepsiCo, it's not enough to know that they "sell soda pop and snack food products." Instead, if you want to stand out from other HR candidates you need a strong grasp of the following:

- **Products (or Services):** What is the specific array of products (or services) that the organization creates? How do they fit with each other?
- **Competitors:** Who are the top 1-2 main competitors? How does the employer differentiate itself from them?
- **Customers/Market:** What are the target customers for the organization?
- **Revenue:** How does the employer generate revenue and make money?
- **Love and Hate:** How do customers feel about the employer's product or service? What do they love or hate? What are the most common complaints and issues?
- **Metrics:** If possible, try to learn about the employer's 2-3 key metrics. Finding exact numbers might be difficult, but you can at least get an understanding of which key business numbers they're doing well on and which ones they're struggling with.
- **News and Rumors:** Have there been any interesting news reports about the employer? What is the organization rumored to do? Don't just read these items. Formulate an opinion about them.

Knowing The Employer's Strategy

You should know not only *what* the organization is doing, but *why* it is doing it. Knowing the "why" will help your answers fit the employer's view of the world and you'll come across like a veteran of the company.

For example, if the employer cares about "providing technology that makes people's lives easier and better" (Apple) then you should mix that sort of passion into your answers. Or if the employer is passionate about "relieving hunger across the nation" (Feeding America), you should talk enthusiastically about that mission.

Knowing the "why" means understanding the following:

- **Mission:** Look up the employer's mission statement. How does it live up to this mission? Be specific.
- **Strategy:** What is the employer's business strategy? How is it currently executing against it?
- **Strengths:** Consider the organization's products or services -- what are their strongest selling points? How does the company leverage those? What about the company or its products has enabled its success?
- **Weaknesses:** What are the major issues, problems and complaints with the organization and its products (or services)? How does it address those weaknesses?
- **Challenges:** What are the biggest challenges for the organization right now? How are they addressing them? What challenges have they recently overcome?
- **Opportunities:** Is there anything on the horizon (with technology or within their industry) that they are capitalizing on?
- **Threats:** Similarly, is there anything on the horizon which might threaten the organization's success?
- **Future:** What do you think the future holds for this employer? Think about any new products or features that would be a natural fit.

Knowing The Employer's Culture

You should develop a good feel for what it's like to work at the organization. This includes:

- **Work Environment:** What is the everyday work environment like? The employer's website homepage might discuss this a little, but that's obviously going to be biased toward the image they want to project. Look further online for articles about what candidates, current employees, and former employees say about working there.
- **Values:** What does the employer value? "Values" pertain to anything that's important to them, explicitly or implicitly. To understand this, read interviews with the founders and think about their culture and products. Val-

ues might include aspects such as "moving fast" (Facebook) or "don't be evil" (Google).

- **History:** How long has the organization been around? How did it get started? Have they been doing what they set out to do, or have they pivoted?
- **Key People:** Who founded the organization? What were they doing previously? If it's a startup, how was it funded? Are there well-known people still employed there? These aren't just "facts" to know; you should think about them. How does the background of the founders and other key people affect the employer?
- **Organization:** How big is the organization? How is it organized? Does everyone basically report to the CEO or is it separated into divisions that operate as separate businesses?

Side Note: If you can, see if you can connect the dots between the business and HR sides of the organization. Let's say you're interviewing with Amazon. They have a reputation for being a low-margin, frugal and metrics driven business. How does this affect their HR strategy? Does this mean that all their HR programs and initiatives must be grounded in metrics and done on the cheap? These are the kinds of preliminary hypotheses you want to draw from your research that make for great questions to pose to your interviewers.

Speaking of which, let's talk about...

Knowing Your Interviewers

Who will you be interviewing with? In addition to your future boss and key members of the HR team, you should expect to be speaking with those who would be your major clients. That is, the key leaders for the group, business unit, division or company that you'll be primarily supporting. For example:

- If you're interviewing for the HR director role for a product line or business unit, you should be talking to the business leader of that unit or line, their finance head and the chief engineer.

- If you're interviewing for a talent acquisition position for the finance division, you should be speaking with the CFO and the key members of the accounting and finance leadership team.
- If you're interviewing for the top HR job, you should be interviewing with the CEO, the CFO, the COO and/or the key operating leaders.

It's a bad sign if you're interviewing only with HR. If your future clients don't think you're important enough to spend time with, that could reflect their attitude about the entire HR function.

And if you don't speak with your key clients and with someone at a higher level than your position, you won't have an accurate picture of what's truly expected of you – which could set you up for failure.

So, insist on speaking with the key people you will be supporting every day. Here are some additional action steps to take in this area:

- **Before your interview, get a list of the people you're meeting with from the company as soon as possible.** Then google their names and check them out on LinkedIn or Facebook.
- **Know their backgrounds and reputations to the extent possible.** This includes what type of behavior might intrigue them or turn them off. Find out everything you can about them: it lowers your stress and allows you to interview more effectively.
- **Capitalize on what you learn. Prep a couple of questions that are specific to each interviewer.** During your interview, work in or highlight a commonality you share, without hitting them over the head with it. Discuss current events on his or her specialty. Or bring up a common interest you know he or she has outside the office. Don't be creepy or too intrusive, though. Congratulating an in-

terviewer on her recent marriage, for example, comes off "stalker-ish" and should be avoided.

Where To Find Information About The Employer

Plow through the employer's website. Go through their annual reports, mission statement, About Us pages, their blog, their SEC filings, newspaper articles, blog articles, individual employee videos, their support pages, and whatever else pops up at their site.

Execute some targeted employer searches on google. Insert the "employer's name" and then words that will bring up the news items and issues such as:
"news"
"quality issues"
"disgruntled staff"
"financial trouble"
"customer complaints"
"poor service"
"bad reputation"
"consumer affairs"

Adopt LinkedIn, Facebook and Google as your new best friends. Use them dig out everything there is to know about the folks you'll be interviewing with. In particular, spend time studying their LinkedIn profiles pages like you've never had anything better to do in your life.

- Did you attend the same school?
- Do you have a common outside interests?
- Do you have common life events (e.g., kids and pets)?

You want to use this information subtly. You don't want to say: "Oh, I looked you up on Facebook and saw that we share an interest in..." That's how you go from candidate to stalker.

Instead, use this info to help you prepare potential conversation starters with your interviewers that you'll only use if they're brought up first by them through pictures on their wall, items on their desk or mentioned by them or others directly.

Talk to your network. Probe current contacts (former bosses, trusted colleagues, clients or relatives) to determine if they have worked there previously or if know any of the individuals on your interview schedule.

Twitter. This can also be an excellent resource because you can see what the company and its employees are talking about. Are they sarcastically bantering with each other? Are they tweeting up a storm about an event or new product launch? Use it to get another pulse reading on the company and its culture (along with any negative press).

Glassdoor, Vault. Use these two sites to surface company reviews from current and previous employees – but take them as a guide, not fact. Often, these sites are dumping grounds for disgruntled employees or created by happy or displeased customers. However, reading enough reviews can reveal some common themes, which can help you come up with insightful questions to ask (and get a sense for whether the answers you get are legit).

Use the product or service. No matter what HR role you're interviewing for you should attempt to use the product or service before your first interview (and ideally, a few times), if possible.

Obviously, this isn't always practical. If it's a consumer product like food, that's easy. If they manufacture and sell equipment for astronauts, it's more difficult. But if you can, it will help you answer the question: "Have you ever used our product (or service)?"

Also, if you're hired, your goal will be to create value and serve clients who work directly on the product or service...and being a user or consumer yourself is the first step in understanding their issues.

Summary

Digging into the employer, their strategy, their culture and your interviewers will increase your confidence and enable you to position yourself as a strong candidate for the job.

This kind of homework will enable you to ask insightful questions and speak very specifically about ways you can contribute to its success from an HR perspective. And all of this will impress your interviewers.

4

ESTABLISH RAPPORT & MAKE A GREAT FIRST IMPRESSION

Now that you've done your homework, you're ready for your interviews. As you walk in and greet each interviewer, there's one little reality you must recognize...

You Have Roughly 30 Seconds To Make A Strong First Impression.

But you already knew that, right?

However, why so little time?

Because for thousands of years, human survival has depended on how quickly we can size up another person or a situation. Our brains are hardwired to evaluate other people quickly (even if we do so inaccurately).

Employers are human. And like all humans they take mental shortcuts when making decisions. Your cover letter is glanced at. Your resume is skimmed. And accordingly, your interview results can be determined in those first few seconds by the initial impression that you create.

So your first step is to immediately establish rapport and to personally connect with each interviewer. If you're naturally introverted, it may seem hard to click with someone you hardly know (or who doesn't seem very likeable) but there IS a way.

That way is to just picture the interviewer as a friend or someone you admire. And then engage in some seemingly *very basic* and *simple* behaviors that you probably use every day as an HR pro in interacting with your clients. They include:

#1: Put The Interviewer At Ease.

If they've not met you before, most interviewers will have anxiety just like you. Some will have perused your resume and are ready for your visit. Others will not have. Nevertheless, most want you to like them and want to leave a good impression. So you can't go wrong by taking a few important but subtle actions towards creating an inviting environment for both of you.

(a) Present a warm smile, no matter how you feel. Direct eye contact and a smile conveys confidence, high self-esteem, competence and enthusiasm. Plus, believe it or not, medical research into brain activity has shown that when people smile, they actually connect better with others and perform *more* effectively because they are using more of both the left and right sides of the brain.

(b) Deliver a firm handshake, using the whole hand. A handshake that's too loose unconsciously communicates passivity. On the other hand, a bone-crushing handshake sends a message that you may be overly competitive. Neither of these messages is attractive to an interviewer.

A handshake that is firm with one, two, or three "pumps" of the elbow is an appropriate business greeting, signaling to the employer, "Let's get down to business." And there is no reason to shake a woman's hand any differently than you would shake a man's hand. Firm and businesslike is the rule to remember.

(c) Greet the interviewer pleasantly. Something simple like the following works in most situations:

Hi Bill, I'm Jenn Gonzales. Thanks for taking the time to meet with me today.

In stating this, you've confirmed who you are (and how to pronounce your name as well as the fact you like to be called "Jenn" not "Jennifer") and that you know whom you are meeting with. Hopefully, you have spoken in a clear voice, not mumbling or rushing out your words. If so, you're off to a strong start!

After the introduction, the interviewer will ask you to sit down. Don't sit until he or she asks you to. If he or she does not ask, say politely, *"May I have a seat, please?"*

All of these little touches will get your interview off to a positive start.

#2: Connect By Sharing Something In Common.

When entering an interviewer's office, notice your surroundings. It may be that you can make small talk about the interviewer's awards on the wall, interesting artwork, pictures of kids, plants, tidy desk, out-of-the-ordinary furniture, and so on. For example:

> If the interviewer's desk is cluttered with family photos, consider saying something like, *"It looks like you've got a budding soccer star there!"*

Another terrific way to share something in common is to comment on the interviewer's background based on the company research you've done. If meeting new people makes you nervous, mentally practice an opener will help you feel more in control.

Here are few examples:

> *"Sally, I've so looked forward to meeting you. I was in the audience and really enjoyed the presentation you gave at the San Diego HR Conference last Fall."*

> *"Kate, very nice meeting you. Jane [your initial contact person] has spoken so highly of you. She tells me you've really made some significant strides with the New Manager Assimilation program. I'll look forward to hearing more about that."*

"Jamal, great to meet you. I read about your company's big announcement of the new ABC acquisition in last week's Wall Street Journal. I hope we'll have time to talk a bit about that."

"Gus, pleased to meet you. I have to tell you that everyone I've met to this point has been nothing but first-class. Your assistant has been especially helpful."

[And, if you have no clue about who the person is] "So glad to meet you. I've been looking forward to better understanding your organization and where I can add value."

#3: Respect The Interviewer's Space.

If it's a cubicle, small office or you are very close to his or her desk, you may feel tempted to put your notepad or some other article like a purse on the desk.

Don't. The desk is the territory of the interviewer, and he or she will feel encroached upon if you pass that invisible line of his or her space and your space. Putting any item, including your hands or elbows on the desk will be taken as a sign of disrespect and an unconscious threat. If you wish to take notes, hold your notebook on your lap.

Also, turn your cell phone off! If you forget and it happens to ring, do not glance to see who called. To show respect, simply apologize for the interruption and turn off the device.

#4: Avoid Looking At Your Resume During The Interview.

Looking is a sign of nervousness, or fabrication. You need to know everything on the resume cold without hesitation. This includes every date, title, and company.

Shooting glances at your resume can also indicate lack of interest or preparation. Regardless of the cause, which is probably due to temporary nervousness or excitement, the interviewer will unconsciously think the worst.

#5: Use The Mirroring Technique.

Mirroring is simply a technique used to strengthen the connection with your interviewer. The principle is to match aspects of your interviewer's voice, mannerisms, and body language. For instance:

- If the interviewer uses hand gestures to explain something, feel free to use hand gestures when speaking.
- If the interviewer leans forward to emphasize a point, subtly lean forward to listen.
- If the interviewer asks questions slowly and softly, respond in a similar volume and pace (but be cautious to not speak too slowly or too softly – you want to convey energy and be audible).
- If the interviewer is cold and business-like and refers to a lot of HR technical jargon, data, and source material, cite data and source material in your answers and don't attempt to win him or her over by being warm and fuzzy.

The point is not to mimic the interviewer like a parrot, but to match his or her style and energy level, without losing your own personality in the process.

Of course, there are some situations where mirroring would not be called for – for instance, if for some reason the interviewer gets angry, defensive or displays any behaviors that wouldn't win an etiquette award, such as slouching or scratching!

#6: Throughout The Interview, Observe The "50-50 Rule."

As mentioned previously, you shouldn't talk all the time. Nor shouldn't let them talk all the time either. Experience has revealed that, in general, the people who get hired are those who divide speaking and listening 50-50 in the interview. Candidates who don't follow that mix are the ones who don't get hired.

If you talk too much about yourself, you risk coming across as self-absorbed and someone who would ignore the needs of the organization. But if you talk too little, you come across as a poor communicator or as someone trying to hide something about yourself. Your interview is a conversation. So keep the conversation balanced.

#7: There's No Need To Save All Your Questions Until The End.

With some interviewers, you can make a more genuine connection by sprinkling a few relevant questions throughout the conversation, instead of saving them all for the wrap-up.

For example, say the interviewer asks you to talk about the most significant accomplishment at your last job. After you speak about your experience leading the "Sales Retention Special Project Team," continue with a question that moves the conversation along, like: *"Retaining our top sales people was one of the major talent challenges we faced. Are there major retention issues you're facing here?"*

By doing that, you'll spark a little back-and-forth conversation, which will not only help you learn more about the company but create a more natural dialog with the interviewer, rather than a very formal, "be-on-your-best-behavior" kind of interaction.

BONUS: Here are TWO more ways to make a great first impression ...even _before_ you arrive at the interview...

#8: Polish Up Your Google Results

In addition to having your LinkedIn profile checked, you should expect to be googled. While you can't totally control your search results, you can do things to improve the chances that they'll be great.

Step one is to google yourself. What do your results show? Are there any comments you've made on social media sites, old embarrassing pictures of you on Facebook or Instagram that you can take down immediately?

Secondly, start improving your online image – especially if it's unflattering. You won't be able to create a new image over-night, but begin now. Start by posting some articles on LinkedIn or on other article sites like ezinearticles.com. Or buy your do-main name (yourname.com) and create a personal website or blog where you can bring together all of your work, experience, and links to other places where you are on the web. If a full-fledged website sounds intimidating, even a simple, single-page site can be enough to own your space on the web.

Finally, make sure that you have updated profiles on all the major social networks – especially LinkedIn, Twitter and Google+. Since these sites are trusted and highly trafficked, Google will rank them highly. Oh, and make sure to use your full name somewhere on all of these sites, as opposed to a user name. Otherwise search engines won't be able to tie them to you.

#9: Get A Recommendation From The Inside.

Do you already know someone at the company you're interviewing with? Even if he or she isn't in HR, a referral from a highly placed leader or executive contact can still be incredibly power-ful. It's proof from someone the organization (and perhaps even the hiring manager) theoretically values that you're good at what you do and potentially a good organization fit.

And what if you don't? Then check LinkedIn to see if you have any mutual connections with the hiring manager or some-one up the HR hierarchy in the organization for which you're applying. If this person is someone that the higher-ups know well, a good word from him or her could have a positive impact also.

Summary

Whether your interviewers are friendly conversationalists or stone-faced interrogators, you absolutely must make a powerful first impression on them. Executing the suggestions in this chapter will help you establish an engaging, memorable, yet personal connection with them fast and will serve as a positive catalyst for the rest of your interview.

5

Interviewer Questions, Part 1:
THE 10 MOST FREQUENTLY ASKED QUESTIONS
YOU ABSOLUTELY MUST NAIL...OR
YOU'RE TOAST!

Let's now move into interviewer questions. Many interview books focus on how to answer the top 100 (or 500) questions.

Puh-lease. Give me a break.

Unless you have a photographic mind, there's no way you can prepare for hundreds of questions. Besides, you're a busy a HR pro, don't have the time – and nor is it necessary

So, we're not going to do that in this book. Instead, in the next three chapters we will cover the three most important categories of questions you'll face in the interview and the special strategies for handling each type.

They include how to successfully address:

1. 10 Most Frequently Asked Questions (this Chapter)
2. Behavior-Based Interview Questions (Chapter 6)
3. Questions That Stump You (Chapter 7)

A few caveats first...

- As you read through the questions, get a feel for them and the language used in the example responses.

- But do yourself a favor: Don't memorize answers, as this will be obvious to savvy, experienced interviewers. And you'll come across as unnatural and phony.
- Finally, whether you have 24 hours or 24 days to get ready for an interview, there's no excuse for not being fully prepared for the questions listed here – even if they aren't asked. Some of them are tough, others are "lay-ups." But don't take any of them lightly. Preparing for all of them will enable you to be as sharp and as confident as you can be.

That said, let's now go through the ten most frequently asked interview questions that you absolutely must get right - or you're history.

Question #1:
"Tell me about yourself."

Other variations of this question:
- Walk me through your resume.
- Take me through your background.

Traps: Beware! Most typical HR interviews begin with this "innocent" warm-up question. Many candidates shoot themselves in the foot by rambling for five minutes or reciting their life story.

Your Strategy: *Unless you're specifically asked to do it, avoid rehashing everything on your resume.* Remember, most interviewers will have already read through it. Those who haven't will appreciate your brevity.

Instead, answer this question with a "MINI-BIO"…
which is a short sound bite, between one to two minutes long that summarizes your background and the three biggest benefits you offer.

You'll find an example template on the next page to help you in creating yours. All you have to do is just fill in the blanks.

Template For Crafting Your "Mini-Bio"

I'm currently with _____ where I've been
for the last _____ years.

I have _____ years of experience as a
_____ in the _____ industry,
specializing in _____ .

I have currently have a [B.S., M.A., certificate] in _____
from the University of _____ and an [MBA,
MSHRM, MS, Ph.D] from the University of _____
at _____ .

I offer three key experiences that I believe are closely aligned to the
needs of the position.

    First, _____ .

    Second, _____ .

    Third, _____ .

I'm here today because I'm excited about what I've heard so far
about the _____ organization and what you're
doing to _____ .

I believe my overall experience as a _____ will
potentially enable me to make a major contribution to
_____ and support objectives of the _____
group.

[Optional] *I'd love to hear more about what you need for this position. For instance,* _____ *?*

Here's an example answer crafted using the "Mini-Bio" template – responding to the question: "Tell me about yourself."

I'd be happy to. I'm currently Director of HR at the Healthy Foods Company in their Orange Juice Division, where I've been for the last three years.

My background includes over seven years of total HR leadership experience primarily in the consumer products industry, specializing in talent management, labor relations and managing employee engagement initiatives. I received my B.S. in Management and M.A. in Psychology at Ohio Wesleyan University – both with honors.

*I offer **three key strengths** that I believe are closely aligned to your Senior HR Director's position in your Wireless Products Division.*

*First, I have strong experience **helping leaders retain their top talent.** Over the last two years, I've collaborated with our divisional executives to improve the retention rate of our top engineers from 85% to 97% -- and did it by developing a unique program that has now been adopted by all six divisions of the company.*

*Second, I'm an excellent **project leader.** I was selected as the HR lead for the corporate-wide task force that merged four fragmented customer service centers into one, single centralized unit. This saved our company over $3.6 million through reductions in headcount and administrative costs.*

*Third, I have a strong **track record in improving employee engagement.** As the site HR leader for our Orange Juice factory, I led initiatives that improved employee engagement index by 12 percentage points and increased our site's ranking from #6 to #2 out of 20 manufacturing locations on our annual survey.*

I'm here today because I'm very impressed with the tremendous growth your company has had in the last two years.

Based on the initial chats I've had with Jill, I'm excited about the position in your Consumer Products Division and believe my HR background matches up well with what you're looking for.

However, I'd love to hear more about what you need for this position. For example, what do you consider the most pressing projects or issues I'd be tackling in the first 90 days on the job?

Key Points about using the "Mini-Bio" template:

- **Customize and tweak it so that it fits the specific position for which you're interviewing.** *All positions aren't the same, so don't give the same canned pitch to each employer.* This is the single most important strategy in successful interviewing. Do all the homework you can before the interview to uncover *specifically* what they're looking for (see Chapter 2, point #10) so that your Mini-Bio hits their hot buttons.

- **When delivering your Mini-Bio, don't go beyond three key selling points.** If you deliver more than three, you'll bury the interviewer in too much information. Talk about fewer than three, and you'll come across as inexperienced.

- **Make the wording work for you.** Your three selling points can be "strengths," "key experiences," "assets," "competencies," "passions" and the like. The wording you use should feel comfortable and sound strong.

- **At the very end of delivering your Mini-Bio, you can also *optionally* transition into a question to help you gather more information about the job**. Note how this is done at the very end of the template and in the example. This is not necessary in all cases, but it can provide info helpful later on.

- Finally, while I don't recommend memorizing answers to interview questions, this is the ONE exception to the rule. Rehearse your Mini-Bio alone in front of a mirror. Or video or audio record yourself. Know it backwards and forwards, inside and out. You want it to deliver it naturally without feeling like you're following a script.

Question #2:
"Why are you interested in this HR position?"

This is your opportunity to hit the ball out of the park and show how your aspirations ideally fit the position.

Traps: If you can, avoid mentioning money. It won't do you any favors even if that's the real reason you want the job. Joining a company for more cash implies you will leave as soon as someone else offers you more.

Your Strategy: Keep your answer focused on the opportunities at this organization. Talk about your desire for:
- a new career challenge,
- an opportunity for advancement,
- the chance to perform at a higher level, and/or
- more recognition for your contributions.

Example #1 – Opportunity for Advancement:

Although I'm performing very well in my current role at Capital Tech, I'm exploring positions that will provide me with more upward growth and that will leverage my extensive experience in managing leadership development programs. This is a key component of your Talent Development Manager position and is exactly what I'm looking for.

Example #2 – Chance To Perform At A Higher Level:

For my HR master's degree project in college, my team built an online HR competency model. I truly enjoyed project work and being part of that team – and received excellent feedback on my contributions. I'm now seeking an HR role that will allow me to take my strong project management and team skills and apply them at the next level. And your HR project analyst position seems to be an ideal role that enables me to do this.

Question #3:
"What is your biggest strength?"

Traps: This seems like a softball question, but be ready. You don't want to come across as arrogant nor humble. While many interviewers have moved away from this basic question, it's still commonplace enough that you should be prepared for it.

Your Strategy: Choose one or more of your strong points and relate them to the opening you're being interviewed for.

Example:

I have a number of strengths that would be of value in the position. However, the one most related to what we've discussed is my flexibility in getting results with tough clients.

I can be strong in pushing for my ideas and I can also flex my approach when the situation changes. I've found that this strong, yet adaptable style has allowed me to build tremendous credibility with tough and demanding clients like those you described in your R&D organization. My clients have come to respect me because they know I'm not a pushover and will always strive to do what's right for their business. And I'm confident I can have similar results with the clients here...

Question #4:
"What is your greatest weakness?"

Other more diplomatic variations of this question:
- What development areas are you currently working on?

- What skills or experiences are you trying to strengthen?

Traps: Don't try to offer up a strength and position it as a weakness. For example, giving answers such as "I'm a perfectionist," or "I'm a workaholic," Just about everyone knows about this tired old tactic – especially savvy, experienced hiring managers and recruiters who will immediately see right through this as disingenuous bull and smoke you out as a phony trying to evade the question.

Let's face it. We all have areas we're working on developmentally as HR professionals. And they're not going to be shocked to discover you have some too – we all do. So I advocate CANDOR and HONESTY.

Here's why. If I'm interviewing you, I'm not your enemy. So don't treat me like one by trying to snow me with BS. If you're a good fit for the HR role I'm interviewing for, I want to find that out and hire you. And if you're not a good fit, I want to find that out too so that I don't put you in a job that you'll struggle with and even risk getting fired from. It's not good for me. And it's definitely not good for you and your HR career – and that's what is MOST important. Assuming I want a great hire and you want to land a position where you'll thrive, HONESTY is more likely to get us both there.

Your strategy: Be open and truthful. To accomplish this without weakening your candidacy, do this:
  (1) Select an area that you have been working on developmentally.
  (2) Describe what you're doing (or have done) to address it.
  (3) Then deliver an answer which covers BOTH (1) and (2).

Three Examples:
- *A few years ago, I found that I wasn't as naturally organized as I wanted to be. It was because I didn't have a system to keep track of my major HR priorities and I'd lose some momentum on them and fall behind. So now I'm addressing it by making "to do" lists on my*

smartphone religiously and check them each morning and afternoon to make sure that absolutely nothing is slipping through the cracks and that all my priorities stay on track. I've improved a lot but I'm still not perfect at this, so I carry my phone with me everywhere, because I know that without having my current priority list at my fingertips, I won't be as organized as I need to be."

- *I used to become frustrated and impatient when the work of other people negatively impacted my own HR projects and initiatives. Now I've come to understand that everyone has a unique contribution to make and I now make an extra effort to help my colleagues with problems they may encounter early in order to expedite our overall team's progress. I've learned that this more cooperative approach will deliver a much better end result in the long run for everyone.*

- *One of the things I'm working on is being overly objective and analytical. It's both my greatest strength and my greatest weakness. Sometimes, I need to weigh the subjective and people implications of my decisions even more than I do. I've been addressing this by making sure I ask for regular input from others – especially members of my team who offer different perspectives. Let me give you an example. There was a situation with XYZ Co. where we needed to cut costs. To me, objectively and analytically, it was clear we needed to lay off three people on my team to achieve this goal. However, I eagerly sought input from several of my direct reports before making a final decision. And their thoughts helped me to see some options that would achieve our financial objectives without doing these cutbacks and jeopardizing the morale and stability of my team.*

Key Points: Each of these examples takes a developmental area you've been working on – disorganization in the first; impatience with people in the second; and being overly analytical in the third – all areas that normally would raise a huge red flags, and instead shows how you have <u>neutralized them</u> as an issue.

Question #5:
"Where do you see yourself three to five years from now?"

This question is designed to test your commitment and ambition. Most people would love to get promoted. However, don't feel compelled to inflate your ambitions simply because you think that's what the interviewing team wants to hear. Not everyone wants to be the CHRO, and not every organization is looking for superstar candidates who will reach that level someday.

I have seen a number of excellent candidates who have told me, *"My passion is compensation and benefits. That's what I want to do and be the best C&B person I can be and to increasingly make a bigger impact throughout my career in that area."* And that's okay. I know many HR VPs who are looking for you.

Whatever it is that you want to do, however high you want to climb in HR, be sure you can speak passionately, authentically and realistically about your career goals.

Traps: Expressing a desire to get promoted at warp speed or describing unrealistic job moves that the employer may be unprepared to make (e.g. *"I want to work here in New York for six months and then apply for a company relocation package to be closer to my relatives in L.A."*). This can create doubts in the employer's mind about whether you will be pleased in the job or with the career path being offered.

Your Strategy: Reassure the interviewer that you're looking to make a serious commitment and that this position matches exactly what you want and do extremely well. As for your future, stress your belief that if you perform with excellence, you would expect to be considered for opportunities to advance your career. No more specificity is needed.

Two Examples:

- *Your position as HR Business Partner for the Sales organization is a great fit. Three to five years down the road, I'm confident that if I over-achieve -- which I plan to do -- more advancement opportunities will inevitably open up. It's always worked that way in my career and I'm confident it can work that way here too.*

- *My passion lies in labor relations and working with manufacturing leadership teams to make them successful. That's my strength and my primary goal right now is to become the best field HR leader I can be. Three to five years from now, I want to grow my career and increasingly make an even bigger impact in this particular area of the business.*

Question #6:
"Why did you leave (or why are you leaving) that employer?"

Uh-oh. Delicate subject. Only insane people voluntarily leave jobs they're in love with. And most interviewers presume there is a problem or you'd probably be looking to stay put...and they want to make darn sure that the problem isn't you.

Your explanation is simple and easy to understand when you've clearly left a position for a better one. However, things get trickier in the following types of situations:

(A) If you're currently employed, but looking elsewhere.

(B) If you've been laid off.

(C) If you were fired.

In these cases, you'll want to develop "**Exit Statements**" (i.e. talking points <u>for</u> <u>each</u> <u>employer</u> <u>for</u> <u>whom</u> <u>you</u> <u>worked</u> explaining your reasons for leaving them). These statements should be brief, factual and not defensive. Below are some example exit statements that fit these three specific situations preceded by their underlying strategy.

Situation A: If you're employed, but seeking a better opportunity...

This clearly is a great position to be in. If you currently have a job, you're obviously in a stronger position than someone who doesn't.

Your Strategy: Emphasize honestly what you're looking for in a new position and why. Any of these reasons, which range from benign to positive, work well as an explanation.

- *Learn more* (if the current job provides no/limited opportunity to learn and grow).
- *Earn more* (if the company has frozen pay, limited promotions or eliminated salary increases).
- *Grow more* (if you wanted to take on more responsibility and couldn't).
- *Work more* (if the current job is temporary or part-time, the company cut your hours or planning to relocate its offices across the country).
- *Commute or travel less* (if you want to spend less time away from home because of your family, caring for a terminally ill loved one, accident/illness, etc.). In this case, avoid revealing too many details, but be factual.

Traps: Again, avoid overly focusing on compensation. It should not be your sole reason for changing jobs, unless you're grossly underpaid. A candidate who is just looking for more money often doesn't make a great employee – and interviewers worry that such candidate lack passion and commitment for the job, and will leave that company as soon as the opportunity for more cash comes up.

Finally, as always, avoid saying disparaging about your current employer, or it will look like you are whining or not taking personal responsibility.

Example exit statements – if you're currently employed:

- *I've had lots of terrific opportunities in my current role as Compensation & Benefits Director for HardCorp, a family-owned business. But in the last three years, the company has not been profitable. I feel very proud that the owners valued my work enough to keep me on board. However, I feel it's now time to explore opportunities at larger, leading edge companies like yours where there are more opportunities for growth. I got very excited when Judy Kramer, who works in HR at your Dallas office, told me about what you've been doing with your sales incentive programs. In my current role, I implemented a popular sales incentive program for our Western Region sales reps that helped drive an increase in revenue in that region by 25% in one year. I'm sure this experience would be valuable to your organization in the Comp & Benefits position we've been discussing...*

- *My company recently relocated its main offices to the far northwest suburbs of Chicago, so the commute is currently over 2 ½ hours each way for me. To lessen my daily travel, I've targeted my HR job search to firms exclusively based in the downtown Chicago area, like yours. In my current role, I've led our company's efforts to fill IT and Marketing positions with high-potential women and Latinos, similar to what you're doing here. I've developed some great contacts in the industry and innovative strategies for sourcing this top talent reducing our time to fill these jobs by 20%. I'm sure this experience can benefit your organization in the Executive Recruiting position we've been discussing...*

<u>Situation B:</u> If you've been laid off...

Welcome to the group. Thousands of brilliant HR people have been laid off due to mergers, acquisitions, consolidations and other market conditions outside of their control. If you've lost your job for these reasons, you can be comforted by the fact that it no longer carries the stigma it once did.

Your Strategy: If you were part of a large layoff, it's important to include numbers. Being one of 15 or one of 2,000 (depending on the company's size) makes it clear you weren't singled out.

You might also want to mention multiple rounds of layoffs. Sometimes companies lay off employees in a series of rounds. The common perception is that the first round of layoffs consists of marginal people the company wanted to get rid of anyway. The subsequent rounds begin to include good employees. If you were in a second or third round of layoffs, mention that in your exit statement.

Example exit statements – if you've been laid off:

- *Due to market conditions, National Automotive has reduced the size of their salaried workforce by 350 positions. I was able to retain my job through the first two rounds of layoffs. However, my HRIS position was eliminated in the third round.*

- *Because of serious financial problems, Tremont Mining underwent a major restructuring and unfortunately, this resulted in the elimination of more than 8 regional HR positions across the entire company, including mine. I'm looking forward to exploring new opportunities.*

- *Due to an acquisition by XYZ Corp, the entire 30-person Learning & Development function was eliminated. Now I'm looking forward to exploring new options for employment. I very much enjoyed the people I worked with and the work that I performed. But I believe that this may ultimately be to my advantage due to the opportunity I see with your company. I know that working for your organization I will have the opportunity to ...*

Situation C: If you were fired...

First things first. You should know that your former employer cannot legally disclose information if you were terminated or say anything negative (or positive) about your performance. The only information that can be legally revealed is:

- Your start date
- Your title at the time of leaving the company
- Your last day with the company

However, even though details about your past work record are legally protected, it's unethical for you to give false reasons for leaving a job to a new employer. If you do, and the truth comes out, you risk termination. But let's face it. HR folks gossip. Stuff happens. Keeping this kind of secret can be a heavy burden to carry. So don't.

Your strategy: *Never lie about having been fired.* Life's too short. Instead, try to deflect the reason from you personally. Examples might be if your firing was the result of a takeover, merger, and division-wide layoff.

However, recognize that the employer's real concern here is whether you were dismissed for lack of performance or an inability to get along with others. And if you fall in this camp and you personally screwed up, <u>say so</u> without degrading yourself or offering excessive details. Talk about the lessons learned from that experience. And find a way to bring this up early on and on your own terms. For instance, when the interviewer is walking through your resume, you might say:

"John, by the way, I want you to know that the reason I left the position that ended in 2011 was because I was asked to leave. Here's what happened...." (Don't blame or complain about anyone.)

Then go on to describe your own firing candidly, succinctly and without a trace of bitterness, from the company's point-of-view. And if you can do so sincerely, indicate that you could understand why it happened and you might have made the same decision yourself. That's the optimal strategy.

Example exit statements – if you were fired:

- *I made an error judgment in how I expressed my disagreement with the direction the company was taking and they let me go as a result. It was a great learning experience for me in terms of how to constructively provide input without alienating me from the management team, and I would certainly handle it differently now.*

- *I took on a set of responsibilities that, in hindsight, I was not prepared to handle and deliver on. It was a great learning experience and taught me to be very honest with myself and others when considering future roles and responsibilities, and to have a realistic assessment as to which roles I'm right for, and which ones are not a fit for me.*

- *I didn't handle a philosophical difference with a colleague well as I should have. And while it resulted in the company and I parting ways, it taught me several valuable lessons around constructive and positive ways to resolve differences with colleagues. If I could go back and do it over again I'm confident I would approach the situation much more constructively and result in win-win for myself, my colleagues, and the company.*

- If you were fired because of a leadership change, describe it without belittling the leader: *"There was a total changeover in senior HR management, which led to me and a number of my colleagues being let go."* If you know how many employees were fired as a result of the leadership change, then state that figure. If it's more compelling stated as a percentage, then express it in those terms – e.g. *"In fact, more than 30 percent of the company's workforce was let go during this period."*

- If it was a personality clash: *"I've been fortunate to work with a number of fine supervisors over the years, and I've had excellent relationships with all of them, except for one individual. I'm disappointed that there wasn't an opportunity to work further on the relationship. You'd probably like to hear some other people's perspective on this as well, and I'm happy to provide you references from that employment period."* (Then, be sure to let your references know that someone may be calling about this.)

Statements like these in the examples will demonstrate consummate professionalism and most importantly you will show you are healed from the wounds inflicted by the firing.

In the eyes of many (not everyone), you will enhance your image as a first-class HR leader and stand head and shoulders above the legions of firing victims who, at the slightest provocation, rip open their shirts to expose their battle scars and decry the unfairness of it all.

Key points:
- **If you were fired, don't try to cover it up.** There's a great chance that they'll find out eventually and things will get ugly.
- **Avoid using hot words.** Words like "personality clash" or "didn't get along" will cast a shadow on your competence, integrity or temperament.
- **Plan to do a little confessing:** *"I have to be honest with you here. That was kind of a bad situation that I'm embarrassed about. It wasn't a good decision to take that job – I did it for the wrong reasons, it wasn't a good fit, etc, etc I can only say that it was a brief bump in the road of an otherwise great career so far..."*
- **Offer up your references.** *I'd love to have you speak to some of my references, including a former manager (a*

great boss from a job you've had in the past). *They will be able to speak to my qualifications for this job, and my work ethic.*" In doing this, be absolutely sure your references are rock solid.

Question 7:
"In looking over your work history, I'm concerned. Can you explain _____?"

Lots of HR folks have less-than-ideal work histories, so don't worry if you do too. You should be especially prepared if any of the following are present in your job history.
    (A) Too many jobs.
    (B) Out of a job for a long period of time.
    (C) Gaps and lengthy periods between jobs.
    (D) Short time in your last job.
Let's take each of these situations, one by one…

(A) Why have you had so many jobs?

Leaving one job for a better one can be a smart career move. But too many jobs in a short time span can signal "job hopper" in the minds of hiring authorities -- and their worst nightmare is hiring you and having to replace you six months later.

How many jobs are too many? In a Robert Half survey, HR executives said that an average of six jobs in 10 years or three job changes in two years can prompt worries you're a serial job changer. In these cases, there's an assumption on the part of the hiring authority that you're going to be at your next job for only one year or less. They worry that you either get fired too often, get bored too easily or just can't seem to pick the right job.

Your Strategy: Talk about how your past roles were either: (a) designed as part of a grand plan to build your experiences for this specific role you're now seeking; (b) took place at much different phase of your career that you've now transitioned from;

or, (c) that this particular role is different because it matches up with roles that you enjoyed the most and remained in the longest. Your real aim here is to take focus away from you being perceived as an indecisive, high-risk hire.

Examples:

- *For my first five years in HR, I explored a number of different roles to help me grow my skills faster and gather critical experiences. They helped provide an important foundation for my career. I'm now extremely clear and comfortable with my direction in the future and I'm absolutely convinced that this particular job is perfect for me in the longer-term for these 3 reasons…*(then describe those reasons).

- *My job changes were more frequent in my younger days when I was single, less experienced and trying to establishing myself in HR. At this stage in my career, I've matured; I'm much more settled and know exactly what I want. I've absolutely fallen in love with working with clients on their talent management issues and helping them grow their businesses. And, I'm excited with the long-term opportunity that this particular position provides to do this with your Marketing & Media groups…*

- *While it's true that I've moved through a variety of roles, the two positions I enjoyed the most and spent the most time in were the roles where I contributed as an HR member of the client's leadership team. That's exactly what has attracted me to this position at your firm and what I'm seeking today…*

(B) Why have you been out of a job for so long?

Don't blame the economy or state of the HR industry. Be upbeat and positive – and emphasize any constructive activities you've engaged in during your period of unemployment.

Best example:

- *I'm taking the time to be very selective. I want to find the right opportunity and the best fit. In the meantime, I've kept busy by doing independent HR consulting work focused on helping small businesses with their hiring and employee relations issues.*

   With respect to the right fit, I've specifically targeted organizations like yours which leverage my strengths as an HR business partner in the hospitality industry where I played a major role in driving business results through people. You mentioned, for instance, that you need an HR generalist who can...

(C) You have a huge gap on your resume between your last two employers. What did you do during that time?

While answering honestly, there's no need to provide more details than absolutely necessary. For example, if the gap was several months to a year, it is fine to be direct and straightforward and mention that you were:

- Taking maternity leave
- Caring for children
- Caring for a terminally ill family member
- Taking time off for travel abroad
- Taking time to pursue or further your education

All of these situations are part of going through life's natural personal and career stages. However, in citing these reasons, be clear that the reason for your hiatus has passed – and emphasize constructive activities you've engaged in during your gap period.

   You want to demonstrate that your HR skills are not stale. So if the time was spent on an entirely in a longer-than-hoped-for job search, be ready to point to some other concurrent activity, such as:

- Doing some HR consulting work
- Taking business- or HR-related classes
- Volunteering in an HR capacity with non-profits or in the community

Example:

- *For the two years, I served as the primary home care provider for my terminally ill mother before she passed away. It required a full-time commitment to her that I'll never regret. However, during the time I cared for her, I also served as a part-time volunteer fundraiser for the Make A Wish Foundation. In this role, I recruited and trained 14 volunteer fundraisers. And I also planned and promoted three successful fundraising events including an auction, dinner and concert which generated over $125,000 in pledges. All of this has helped me keep my recruiting and business skills sharp...*

Key points: If you have been out of work for an extended time, don't be defensive or discount the gap with the attitude that, "it's no big deal." It is a very big deal, especially to the employer. Simply tell the truth with facts and humility.

(D) Why did you work for your last company such a short time?

You may have simply changed your mind about working there, but you need to provide a *solid reason.*

Best answers:

- If the employer is the reason: *The company was in financial trouble and reduced the workforce...*

- If this wasn't the case: *The job responsibilities were dramatically changed once I came on board, and didn't offer the level of responsibility that was originally intended...*

When answering, remember the options for leaving an employer from Question #6, Situation A cited before - to *learn* more, *earn* more, *grow* more, *work* more, and *commute or travel* less.

Keep reasons simple. The briefer the better. This is not a time to blabber. Only give pertinent information, and do not go into detail. Long explanations make you sound as if you're being defensive and covering up something. If the interviewer wants more detail, he or she will ask for it.

Question #8:
"What are your salary expectations?"

Answering this question too early in the interview process is risky. If you reveal too high a dollar figure, you'll be eliminated before you are considered. But if you state too low a number, then you can get low-balled. It can be a lose-lose situation.

However, even with all that said, I recommend that you don't play coy or sidestep the question. That will just frustrate the hiring authority. And frankly, you don't need to waste your time either on a position beneath your compensation expectations.

So when asked, provide a **salary range**, rather than one hard number. Base it on the high and low spectrum of your desired salary with the expectation that you'll ultimately land somewhere in middle. In doing this, make very clear that the amount depends on the robustness of benefit package and the career trajectory provided by the position, so you still have room to negotiate the dollars later.

Examples:

- *I'm looking for a base salary in the range of $85,000 to $100,000 per year. The exact amount will depend on the* *full benefits package and any potential transition costs related to this job.*

- *Based on relocating to the New York area, I'm seeking a $175K to $200K base, plus bonus, stock and benefits However, salary while important, is not my first consideration. I am much more interested in finding the right position, where I can make a real contribution."*

- *I'm looking for my annual salary to be in the $150K to $180K range, depending on the bonus, benefits, perks and the growth potential provided by the position.*

Again, you're looking for a response that gives you plenty of wiggle room to negotiate the best potential job offer later. Recognize that as soon as you give a number, the employer will try to hold you to it. So, make sure your top number is more than you expect, while the bottom number is a manageable amount if the job came with great perks.

Remember that *your base pay is not the only thing you're negotiating.* You'll be negotiating for a full compensation package that may include a sign-on bonus, extra benefits and perks, and many additional items we'll talk about later in Chapter 13.

Exception: With headhunters, it's okay to reveal your EXACT salary information so they can work aggressively on your behalf. Most of them won't continue a conversation with you if you aren't forthcoming about your current salary and your expectations anyway. So feel free to share this with them, along with any other factors that might influence your request, such as an upcoming bonus or a two-year salary freeze at your company.

Question #9:
What is the most significant project you have led or accomplished in your career?

Your strategy: Don't be modest! This should absolutely be your biggest, boldest, signature initiative. The interviewer is looking to assess the size and scope of your top HR achievement to date, as well as gain clues about your drive, capacity and energy.

Depending on your position and years of experience, the example you provide may be something like a major HR project you launched or led proactively, or it may be a big idea that you suggested that was implemented and adopted by others.

Frankly, if you have two or more years of human resources experience, this shouldn't be a problem. So, let me shift gears. Just to show how just about any aspiring HR pro can effectively respond to this question, **below is an example for a new college grad with no HR experience,** seeking an entry-level HR position:

> *"A number of achievements come to mind, such as proactively completing my degree in three and a half instead of four years and leading a United Way fund-raiser for my sorority that raised $10,000.*
>
> *However, I'd have to say, though, that the accomplishment I'm most proud of that relates most to your HR analyst position is participating as the only undergraduate member of Search Committee that hired the new Dean of the Business School. It was a great honor being picked for this prestigious committee and it taught me a lot about HR essentials such as panel interviewing, creating selection criteria and assessing candidate qualifications. Let me explain further..."*

Note the key phrases bolded above and how they were used to frame the response. Use them in crafting yours as well.

Question #10:
"What makes you the best fit for this job? Frankly, you seem to have too much (or not enough) experience."

This simple question is typically asked at the end of the interview and can be a killer if you're unprepared for it. If you respond with a long pause, stammer, or seem uncertain about your answer, you've blown it.

Let's deal with both the "not enough experience" (Situation A) and "too much experience" (Situation B) questions.

Situation A: If you're viewed as not having enough experience or "too light" for the position...

Your Strategy: Don't get into debates over your experience! Instead focus on selling the experience you DO have. Here's how: If the interviewer hasn't yet told you what they're really looking for, then find this out *first* –and *then* respond to this question, addressing their primary need.

However, if you already know what their main hot button is, then go ahead and pick out one of your strongest accomplishments, competencies or assets that matches what they want (perhaps even from your Mini-Bio) and then add the tagline, *"And that's exactly what I'd like to do and what makes me a strong candidate for this position..."*

Example #1:

"Before responding to that question, I'm wondering if you'd tell me a little more about the most important quality you're looking for most in the ideal candidate.

[After the interviewer responds, say...]

Great, that's very helpful. It sounds like we're definitely on the same page.

*First of all, as I understand your primary need, you are first and foremost looking for an HR change agent to play a lead role in selling your non-union employees on needed changes to their benefit plans. **And that's what I've been doing for the last two years.***

In my role as Employee Benefits Manager at KeyCorp, I took charge and led the effort to restructure hourly benefit programs across four locations...resulting in $2.4 million in annualized savings for the company....and I worked hard *with the HR leadership team to get employees to buy-in and did so without a disruption in the business. **And that's exactly what I'd like to do for this company and what makes me a strong candidate for this position.***"

Example #2:

From what Roger (the hiring manager) *indicated, the HR department is under tremendous pressure to hire 35 new store managers in the next 90 days before the new apparel stores open. **And filling key positions quickly is precisely what I've been doing for the last few years.***

*As the Talent Acquisition Manager at Rossex, I've used my headhunter contacts and social media resources like LinkedIn and Twitter to attract candidates to fill important jobs in record time – and even convinced many top-notch passive job candidates to change jobs and join us! I won our company's Chairman's Award for HR Excellence for my work in this area. **And that's exactly what I'd love to have to opportunity to do this for this company in this position.***

Key Points:
- The first example illustrates what to do if you're unsure of the primary need. Rather than rattle off an answer blindly, pose a question back to the interviewer to get helpful info about the job before answering.
- The second example references a conversation held with the hiring manager and provides the basis for the response. So asking the question was unnecessary.
- Both answers demonstrate an ability to think on your feet which will scores points in the mind of interviewers. This is not difficult if you've prepared beforehand.
- Whether your interviewer asks you this particular question explicitly or not, this is the most important question of your interview because she must answer this question favorably in her own mind before you will be hired.

Situation B: If you're viewed as having too much experience and/or overqualified for the position...

Their concern in this case is that you'll bolt the organization as soon as something better comes your way. Anything you can say to show your commitment and reassurance of your desire to stay for the long-term will help you overcome this objection.

Your strategy: Don't apologize for being overqualified. Sell it as your biggest asset for the job and why the company is the perfect match. They may not always grasp this on their own.

Examples:

- *"Some people might have concerns about my extensive experience. However, I see that as a big advantage to both myself and for you as my potential employer. I'll be able to get up to speed faster, I'll make fewer mistakes and I'll bring a level of expertise and insight that other HR candidates won't. So your department will benefit big if I'm chosen for this position and I'm extremely excited about this opportunity.*

   However, there was probably something in my resume that interested you enough to call me in. I'm curious, what was that?" (Then, speak further to any other specific experiences and how they will bring extra value to the company...)

- *I think my substantial experience is a good thing. I personally want to be as overqualified as I can for any job I go after. The performance bar is rising all the time and most employers are demanding more value from their HR professionals. With my experience, I offer that additional value. My goal is to be a valuable resource, bringing my years of experience and extensive knowledge to the job and applying them to the challenges you've outlined in this position...*

Special Tips for Older HR Candidates

The use of the term "overqualified" is often "code" for other issues …namely your age.

Age presents a special challenge. Believe it, or not, some HR job seekers are reporting age bias and discrimination beginning as early as the *mid-thirties.*

And by the time you reach your *mid-forties,* you can be considered washed up in some HR departments or by some hiring authorities (though don't expect anyone to tell you this directly).

And if you're *over age 50* interviewing for some HR positions can be rough sledding, if not impossible.

No savvy interviewer is going to come right out and say: "Aren't you too old for this position?" Instead, if they want to know your age, they'll go right to the "Education" section of your resume and simply do the math.

Strategies for dealing with ageism can be complex and personal. One approach is to not reveal any information that will prejudice your chances of getting the offer. To some, I know, this can be extremely insulting. They are justifiably proud of themselves and perceive that concealing facts as playing up to the bigots. This is perfectly understandable, and that is where personal choice comes in.

To that end, here's my advice:

- **On your resume and application, avoid dates.** Be careful how far back in your job history you go. You don't have to have list dates of graduation or your very first HR job. As long as everything on your resume is true, it's fine to leave out something (such as older years of employment). Most employers don't care about jobs held more than 15 years ago. They are more interested in "what have you done lately" and "what can you do for me now." So concentrate primarily on your recent career. If you feel compelled to delve into earlier experiences, create a section called "Early Career" and provide just the highlights and no dates.

- **Appearance and demeanor:** Make sure your wardrobe and eyeglasses are in style. Consider touching up your hair a bit to cover gray and, men, eliminate beards or mustaches, as these often add years to your appearance. Use language that is up to date and have a basic knowledge of contemporary HR trends. Check that your attitude doesn't scream stuffy or outdated.

- **If you're highly compensated,** you can say: *"My major objective is an interesting challenge and money is secondary to that."* Then discuss how you can add value.

- **If there is concern about your health,** you could say: *"I can assure you that I have many productive years ahead of me. The benefit of my experience is that I can hit the ground running and at the same time be a great resource to your more junior, less experienced HR staff."*

- **If there is concern about your having outdated HR skills or your receptivity to change and new technology,** don't come across as a relic or technophobe. Show that you've kept up with the times by removing dated programs and initiatives from your conversation and highlight your knowledge of modern, state-of-the-art HR practices that you've led. You could say: *"I find that over the years, my technology skills have been a consistent strength. I welcome every new HRIS improvement and software introduction. I keep up with the latest HR technological advances because I've found they enable me to perform my job faster and more effectively.*

- **If asked about retirement,** you could say: *"I plan to follow in my father's foot steps. He worked into his 90s! I have absolutely no plans to slow down, as I know myself and know that action and results are what I thrive on. I look forward to being a strong contributor for a number of years to come."* Otherwise, completely avoid the topic of retirement.

- **If asked about getting along with younger coworkers,** you could say: *"I enjoy working with and learning from my younger coworkers, as well as sharing with them* *what I know about executive compensation and talent development strategies. I've reported to someone in the past who was younger than me, and I know this person would say that we had an excellent working relationship. My most important goal is getting results, not recognition."*

Special Note: Clearly, all of the previous example statements won't apply to you. They're just offered simply as illustrations. Adapt them so they fit your situation.

But don't shoot the messenger. My goal is to have the executives who are interviewing you to focus on your results, accomplishments and what you bring to the party...*not to get hung up on your age!* It's also worth remembering that, just because one person who interviews you may be biased, it doesn't mean everyone else is.

Summary

The ten frequently asked questions covered in this chapter are crucial! Even though you probably won't be grilled on all them, you must be thoroughly familiar with them and how you'll respond if you want to outperform and dazzle in your interview.

To help you remember key concepts, jot down and review a few key words for each answer. Rehearse your answers frequently, and they will come to you naturally.

Finally, you're not perfect, so don't try to be. So if you don't perform as well as you'd like on one particular question stay poised, professional and focused...and follow the rest of the principles of successful interviewing presented throughout these pages...and you'll get excellent results.

6

Interviewer Questions, Part 2:
ANSWERING QUESTIONS WHICH ALLOW YOU TO SELL YOURSELF IN A COMPELLING & MEMORABLE WAY

The Three Bears...Hansel & Gretel...Snow White...The Three Little Pigs. What do these all have in common?

They are all short stories. Stories that we all fondly remember from our childhood. Each of these stories is different and unique. Even after decades, I'll bet if you were pressed you could recall the essence of each these stories. And...

The Same Is True Of Conveying A <u>Good Story</u> In HR Interviews.

People will retain your ideas more easily if they're presented in the form of a story. Stories can leave positive impression about you that the interviewer will remember long after your interview is over.

For example, if an interviewer asks about your HR leadership abilities and you simply remark that "you're a strong leader," that's a blah answer because there's nothing to support it.

However, if you tell a story drawn from your experience to describe how you displayed leadership to overcome a significant problem for the organization, it can paint a vivid picture and provide concrete evidence about your leadership skills that can be compelling.

There's another reason stories work so well. After interviewing multiple candidates for a specific position, it's tough for interviewers to distinguish one candidate from another unless one of them – that'll be you – really grabs their interest in a significant way. Your stories are your **secret weapon** for doing this since no one has the same experience or narrative as you do.

But, when should you use them?

Stories Are Most Effective When You Are Asked <u>Behavior-Based Questions</u> Requiring That You Prove Yourself Or Validate Your Credentials.

Typically these types of questions will begin with:
"Give me an example of...?"
"Tell me about a situation where you...?"
"How would you best illustrate your skill in handling...?"
"What evidence can you provide that you can...?"
"What in your background relates to...?"

When these questions are posed to you, it's your opening to launch into a story that can beef up your candidacy and highlight your value.

How To Craft Stories That Are Compelling and Memorable

It's simple.

You follow a straightforward, three-step formula. And that formula is called the **CAR story-telling technique.** CAR stands for C̲hallenge, A̲ction and R̲esult. Here's how it works:

First, describe the <u>Challenge</u>.
This is the situation that you've handled well. It could be a problem (something went wrong) or an opportunity (a potential improvement you identified, neglected by others). But either way, it's your starting point.

Then, talk about the <u>Action</u> you took.
This is where you talk about what you did to solve that problem or capitalize on that opportunity.

Finally, outline the <u>Result</u>.
This is the outcome of the action you took. If possible, it should be presented in terms of numbers, so that your impact is clearly understood. (For example, *"the employee recognition program I initiated led to a 5% reduction in turnover over the next year."*)

However, sometimes numbers won't be available. And if that's the case, just describe the result in words (for example, *"the client was completely satisfied with my solution and wrote a thank you letter to the CHRO."*)

Also, when using CAR, feel free to substitute words that better fit your situation. The word *solution* can be substituted for action. You can also substitute other synonyms for results, such as *outcomes, contributions* or *impact.*

Here's An Example of The CAR Technique In Action.

Let's say your interviewer asks you: *Give me an example of a tough HR problem you solved in your last job?*
Below is how you'd answer using CAR:

Describe the CHALLENGE:

"We were facing a horrible problem in keeping good frontline people in our Customer Service Division. The pay wasn't great and fielding customer complaints all day was no fun. It got to the point where our turnover rate was 10% a month.

Replacing the people who left cost the company an estimated $2.5 million in recruitment and training costs and created terrible morale issues not only in our Apparel Division, but among our customers as well. Everyone was distressed about this situation."

Convey the ACTION you took:

"I worked with the leaders and employees of the department to do an extensive turnover analysis to determine the real root cause of the problem. It turns out that the big problem was that customer service training was inadequate, work hours were too long and they didn't feel valued. To address these issues, we created a Customer Service Success Series of training sessions held every week.

They covered sessions not only on how to handle difficult customers, but it even went beyond this. We provided sessions on managing your career, handling work life balance, saving for retirement and other issues of interest to the customer service reps.

It was the first time anyone had really paid attention to them. We also adjusted their work hours by creating brand new customer service teams, flexible work schedules and rotating shifts that we'd never used before."

Pinpoint the RESULT:

"About two months after these changes were initiated, turnover dropped from 10% a month to 3.7% a month. Even though we invested $200,000 in all the new training and other changes, we wound up saved the company $1.2 million the first year. Morale has drastically improved by 30% based on the last employee survey we did and customer complaints are now at a five-year low.

This overall effort has been well-received throughout the organization and by our customers. And what's really great is that now other divisions have contacted me about addressing morale and talent retention issues with their customer service people as well. I'm ecstatic about what we've been able to achieve."

What is the interviewer likely to infer from this story?
- When faced with difficult issues, you're a problem solver and solution provider.
- You analyze situations, rise to the occasion and get results.

And this is exactly how you want him to react. Now you get to lead them into a natural discussion on the similarities between what you've done and what they need. Make sure you prepare a few more anecdotes to reinforce your positive attributes.

See how this works?

Your CAR stories should take no more than 2 minutes to describe. By structuring your response this way, you paint a vivid and compelling picture of what was going on, what steps you took and what the result was. And you come across as a very desirable and compelling HR job candidate in the process.

Having CAR success stories like this one in your back pocket during interviews work big time. Frankly, even if your success story isn't related directly to the question, you can find a way to adapt it so that it does.

How Many Stories Do You Need?

You need prepare an arsenal of 6-10 killer stories. Now you won't use all of them. But you should have them ready ahead of time.

Struggling to identify some stories? Relax, we all have them. Even if you're a recent college grad, you can use things you did in college to develop stories that present you favorably. If you're a stay-at-home mom returning to the workforce, use things you did at home or while volunteering to develop stories. The key is not to assume that your story has to be a huge company-wide breakthrough worthy of inclusion in the pages of *HR Executive*. It can be a relatively small-scale success as long as it conveys your skills in a compelling way.

Ideally you should prepare <u>at least</u> ONE story for each of the following five types of questions:

1. **Questions About Your <u>Influence & Leadership</u> Skills**
2. **Questions About <u>Challenges</u> You've Faced**
3. **Questions About <u>Mistakes & Failures</u> You've Made**
4. **Questions About <u>Successes</u> You've Experienced**
5. **Questions About Your <u>Teamwork</u> and Collaboration**

Sure, several of your stories may fall under two or more categories. But this is valuable too because you can use a story…even if it doesn't fall into the area you originally intended it for. That said, let's talk more about these five types of questions and where you can find stories that fit and work.

Influence & Leadership Questions

Influencing your clients and leading others are perhaps the most essential skills in HR. You can expect questions to come up often in this area, because most HR positions require getting support and buy-in from others – especially those over whom you don't have direct authority.

Sample Questions
1. *Describe an HR decision you made (or didn't make, but had to implement) that wasn't popular. How did you handle executing it?*
2. *Describe a time when you had to motivate employees or colleagues to accomplish a significant HR/business objective or task.*

3. *Tell me about a time when you had to give a presentation to a group of people on an HR initiative or program they disagreed with.*
4. *Tell me about a time when you had to sell another person or team on your idea.*
5. *Tell me a time where you've built a team – and how you went about accomplishing it.*

To develop potential stories that address these types of questions, think back to times when you've influenced other people, whether it was a client, your boss, colleague, or teacher. What strategies, tactics and techniques worked for you? For example, it could be things like:

- Listening to understand and address the other person (or team's) underlying motivations and needs.
- Getting buy-in from a core group of key team members first and then leveraging that to get other people on your side.
- Being authentic and showing your own vulnerability to encourage others to show theirs.
- Being a good role model or example.
- Gradually leading people to a conclusion by agreeing on a common ground first.
- Developing credibility and engendering trust.

Challenge Questions

Questions about the challenges you've faced are not so much about the actual challenge itself (although it should be something meaningful) – but are asked so the interviewer better understands how you approach addressing tough issues and problems inherent in the HR job for which you're interviewing.

Sample Questions

1. *Tell me about a situation where you had to confront a challenging and demanding client. How did you approach the situation and how was it resolved.*

2. *Tell me about a time when you weren't able to reach an important deadline. What did you do?*
3. *Describe a major change that occurred in a job that you held. How did you adapt to this change?*
4. *Tell me about a time when you had to deal with a significant change in HR or business priorities. How did you handle it?*
5. *Tell me about a time when you had to make a decision quickly or with insufficient data.*

To identify relevant stories you can use to address these types of questions, consider your past experience with the following:

- Client, cultural or work style conflicts.
- Ethical dilemmas.
- Insufficient resources (time, money, expertise).
- Incomplete or inaccurate information.
- Low morale, interpersonal issues, or other emotional problems (with teammates or the team as a whole).
- Changing demands.
- Inability to accomplish a task or meet expectations.

Mistake & Failure Questions

At least one of your interviewers is likely to ask about your past failures or mistakes.

Sample Questions
1. *Tell me about a time when you made an embarrassing mistake.*
2. *Tell me about an HR project or initiative that you failed to deliver on.*
3. *Tell me about a time when you improperly analyzed a situation.*
4. *Tell me about a time when you were disappointed with yourself.*

5. *Tell me about a time when you were unable to success-fully juggle all your HR responsibilities.*

Your interviewer will be looking for the following:

- **A big failure:** Your interviewer wants to see that you've truly failed before. Right or wrong, many leaders believe that if you haven't failed then you haven't really tried. No one is perfect all the time. Thus, counter intuitively, you need to have a substantial failure under your belt.
- **Humility and authenticity:** Your interviewer is also in-terested in determining if you can admit failure. They know that you've failed at some point in your life. But can you admit it, even in a sensitive moment (such as an interview)? Or will you try to sugarcoat it? You want to come across as genuine and sincere.
- **Your handling of the situation:** Did you correct the mistake for that incident, or do something to prevent fu-ture incidents? How did you relay the information to your manager and/or team? What did you learn from it? These are the key insights the interviewer will be looking to gain.

One way to come up with good stories for this category is to think about the things you've learned in your career; often there was a mistake that prompted the learning. For example, maybe you worked hard to create an innovative HR program exactly what your client asked for, but they didn't use it. This may have taught you that you need to dig into your clients' deeper motiva-tions. Stories like this can be great because they naturally lead into the positive ending: you learned something important that makes you a better HR pro now.

Some candidates can go too far though, and their failure amounts to a "red flag." If your answer involves doing some-thing grossly wrong, came close to violating company policy or cuts into your honesty or integrity -- then pick something else. It's fine to have made a mistake analyzing data or trying to take on too much. But if you lied or cheated, your story will only undermine your candidacy.

Success Questions

These kinds of questions are your time to shine. Your answers here might well overlap with your answers to some of the other questions, but that's okay. Your success might be a big challenge you conquered, a time when you led a team to a successful outcome or even a situation where you overcame a potential mistake or failure.

Sample Questions
1. *Tell me about the one accomplishment in your last job that you're most proud of.*
2. *Tell me about a time when you went above and beyond the call of duty and accomplished more than what was expected of you.*
3. *Describe a time when you resolved an HR situation before it became serious.*
4. *Tell me about a time when you had to show innovation and solve a problem in a creative way.*

For these questions, think about the things that you are most proud of.
- Why are you proud of this action?
- Is it because it was especially complex and challenging?
- Was it because it had a huge impact on your company?
- Was it because it was outside of your comfort zone?

Any of these areas can help you develop a fantastic answer. But the key is to pick something that is meaningful to you.

Make sure you can explain to the interviewer why you see this as a success. If it's because it had a big impact on your organization, you should be able to quantify the impact. If it was outside your comfort zone, this should have changed you professionally in some small way or helped you discover something about yourself personally. If it's about solving a vexing problem, you should have learned something significant.

Teamwork Questions

Teamwork questions are used to assess your skills in collaborating, particularly at times when you are working with your immediate peers. Look for instances in your work experience where interpersonal communication or differences in work style affected your team's dynamics.

Sample Questions
1. *Tell me about a time when you had to work across teams to accomplish a significant HR objective.*
2. *Tell me about a time when you were asked to mentor or provide guidance to a team member.*
3. *Tell me about a time when you had to resolve a conflict or compromise with another team member.*
4. *Tell me about a time when you had a challenging interaction with multiple team members who didn't agree with your point of view.*

Stories you can share which address these questions include situations where you have:
- Forged compromises across people.
- Found ways of making your teammates feel valued.
- Been able to agree to things that are suboptimal for you in the interest of the greater team good.
- Understood people's underlying motivations and incentives.
- Motivated teams and boosting morale.
- Relinquished your ego and encouraging others to do the same.
- Balanced autonomy with team cohesion.
- Built the confidence of those around you.
- Set a good example.
- Took personal responsibility.

- Showed compassion and empathy for colleagues.
- Identified and divided responsibilities.
- Shared knowledge and responsibilities.
- Mitigated the damage from a negative teammate or situation.
- Built trust across the team.

There is no "right" way to foster positive teamwork. Part of delivering an excellent answer to these types of questions is understanding that good teamwork is situational.

Additional Key Points About Selling Yourself With Stories and Answering Behavioral-Based Questions:

#1: Expect follow-up probes.

Once you've answered the initial behavioral question, expect that series of follow-up questions will be asked. For example, if asked to: *Describe a situation when you had to successfully lead a team despite significant issues and obstacles standing in the way?"* expect additional probes such as:

- What was your specific role?
- Who else was involved?
- How did the organization react?
- What did you learn from this?
- What would you do differently if this situation came up again?
- Do you always handle situations like this? If not, what made you handle things this way this time?

Listen to these follow-ups carefully as they are often used to dig deeper to verify information or fill in a gap in your initial response. If you see that the interviewer is satisfied with the response, allow him or her to move on to the next question.

If you feel the interviewer is looking for additional information, you can ask, *"Have I fully answered your question?"* However, use this technique sparingly, as asking it too often may signal that you are unsure of your responses.

#2: Speak in bullets.

I've had clients joke that it seems like most HR folks speak in bullets, as though they're always doing a PowerPoint presentation. This isn't a bad thing. In fact, speaking in bullets can be effective.

When you're speaking to an interviewer about an experience you had, they have far less context than you. So to keep them from getting lost in the details of your story, you might want to frame your answer as follows:

- *"I did three things. First, I talked with ... Second, I ... And third, I ..."*
- *"We had two issues with this plan. Number one, we ... And number two, we ..."*

The way to do this is to picture what you say in a bullet list and deliver it that way. That way, your interviewer will have a much easier time following along and embracing your story.

#3: Highlight the role you played within the team.

Being a good team member or leader is a critical skill in today's collaborative organizations. However, the company is not hiring your team – it's hiring you. Team-oriented candidates are often hesitant to take responsibility for a team's success, and during interviews they talk about how "the team did this" and "the team did that."

An interview is not the place to be a good team member and share the glory. If appropriate, you should mention that it was a team effort, but then speak to **what you specifically did** to achieve the results. Don't take credit for tasks performed by others, but don't shy away from detailing and highlighting your outstanding contributions either.

#4: Quantify your results where possible.

This should be the dramatic finale to your story; it should answer the question, "Okay, so you did these things – so what?"

Your results should communicate clearly the success you achieved through your actions and by overcoming the barriers. Depending on how you are feeling and your personality, you can begin the results section with, *"And I'm proud to say...."* Or, you can use a more straightforward, *"And as a result ...."*

If possible, use numbers, which provide credibility and give a scope to the story. Numbers don't have to be dollars; they can be time savings, numbers of people, or numbers of locations. Also, include any recognition you received, whether formal or informal: *"Out of 300 employees in my division, I received the Employee of the Month award for the project."* or *"The general manager wrote a congratulatory note about my performance to her leadership team and to my boss."*

#5: Not all your stories need 100% perfect endings.

Let's be honest. If all your stories have fantastic outcomes, you risk not being believed. Look, senior HR folks know that all too well that every single HR situation can't be solved ideally. So don't try to BS them. They've been in the trenches and on firing line themselves. They have their own stories to tell. But they also know that if you haven't screwed up, got knocked on your butt a few times, misjudged a situation or faced unexpected resistance, you probably haven't been growing.

Savvy and experienced interviewers look for not only what you did (the outcome) but more importantly, *how you did it (your process)*. Specifically:

- They want to make sure that when you come aboard, you're equipped to handle conflicts, challenging and tough HR situations appropriately and in the best way possible under the circumstances, even if the outcome isn't always an ideal one in the short-term.
- They'll also want to know that you didn't have to violate some company norms, betray some confidences or take some high-risk shortcuts in the process. These are no-no's.
- Most importantly of all, they want to know that you learned from your experiences, even (or especially) the bad ones. So in conveying your stories, if you occasionally mention that *"If I had done X just a little bit differently, I would have come out with an even better*

outcome than I did" you've struck gold…and that statement alone can buy you tremendous credibility points and elevate you in the minds of many interviewers.

Look, no one's perfect. You don't have to fake stories. Being authentic, real and slightly imperfect is called being human -- and can be one of your most endearing and compelling assets. Use it.

Summary

CAR stories are a powerful part of your interviewing arsenal. They are excellent for answering behaviorally-based or *"Tell me about a time you…"* types of questions.

The best people I've ever hired in HR all used stories to impress me and knock my socks off. Their stories gave their resumes life. They gave me a clear idea of who they were, how they interacted with others and how they might have handle different situations. They also added layers of depth to their personality and character. Achieving this is the sole purpose of any interview. You want to leave your interviewer with a clear picture of who you are and what you are all about.

Given the success with behavioral/competency-based interviewing, it's likely you'll encounter at least a few behavioral questions if not a 100% full-blown behavioral interview. Welcome this because it will allow you to share stories that make you unique and incredibly attractive as an HR candidate.

7

Interviewer Questions, Part 3:
SUCCESSFULLY DEALING WITH QUESTIONS
THAT CONFUSE OR STUMP YOU

Sometimes hiring managers ask questions they know will throw you off your game. When posing these questions, they aren't as interested in your answer as they are in how you handle pressure and think on your feet.

For example, one of my former colleagues was once asked two bizarre, offbeat questions in an interview by a vice president of Organization Development, who was the hiring manager. They were:

> **"What sea animal best represents your approach to working with your clients and business partners?"**

> **If you could be a superhero, what super-power would you possess?**

Clearly, there was no right answer to these questions. And the hiring manager probably didn't care what her answers were, but was only trying to knock my colleague out of her comfort zone, test her poise, creativity and perhaps even her sense of humor.

Or maybe he was just weird.

Who the hell knows?

My colleague clearly didn't.

All she knew was that she never saw these questions coming and was caught off guard. Frozen with fear and not pausing to think, she embarrassingly stumbled and stammered through her answers. To this day, she couldn't tell you how she responded...only that she didn't get a job offer and left completely pissed at the interviewer and the organization.

Imagine feeling her frustration during your job interview. You've prepared like crazy. And you're already tense enough without worrying that you won't even be able to piece together a coherent sentence. Yet, it's not unusual to find yourself caught in a situation where the right answer just isn't coming to you. Even if you're not tongue tied, you just flat out don't know how to answer an interviewer's question.

What do you do when this happens?

Below is a three-step approach for responding to interview questions that confuse or stump you. This approach can be helpful especially when answering:

- Strange or bizarre questions
- Illegal or unlawful questions
- Questions you're clueless about

Step 1:
Before responding, take your time and acknowledge the question.

First things first. Don't panic. Acknowledge that the question was asked and that you're thinking about it by saying something like:

"Hmm...that's an interesting question. I've not been asked that question before. Let me think about that...

Or if you're confused by the question, you might acknowledge it by repeating the question back or by asking that the interviewer further clarify it. For example:

- *Jim, let me make sure I'm clear on what you're asking. You'd like me to describe which part of a laptop that most reflects my style as an HR leader. Is that right?*

- *Andrea, I'm not exactly sure what you mean by your question about my medical history. Would you mind rephrasing it or giving me a bit more clarification as to the intent of your question?*

These tactics will buy you more time to work through your initial thoughts on the question. Then just pause, breathe and take a few moments to collect yourself and make sure you don't blurt out anything that gives away the fact that you're – well, completely stumped.

Most interviewers know when they've asked you a tough question and will appreciate your thoughtfulness, rather than hearing you ramble through an aimless response filled with verbal junk (e.g., "ums" or "likes").

A little bit of silence won't hurt you here and will provide the time you need to formulate an effective answer. And with more seconds to think, if you're able then to respond to the question, that's absolutely fantastic. However, if you're still stumped, move on to the next step.

Step #2:
If you're still stumped, respond by <u>redirecting</u> your answer to emphasize one of your strengths.

The idea here is that if you're still clueless after buying some time, don't respond directly to the question. Instead, respond by *redirecting your answer* to highlight one of your most significant assets – it could be one of your HR competencies, your experience, the research you've done on the employer, anything – by using variation of the following:

"I'm not familiar with [the question], however I do know [emphasize your big asset]..."

To clarify how this "redirection" technique works, let's take a look at a few examples:

Example #1: Redirecting your answer to highlight one of your biggest strengths.

Let's say you're stumped by that oddball superhero question about what superpower you'd want, here's how you might redirect it emphasize one of your strengths: ***"I'm not very familiar*** *with superheroes or their powers,* ***however, I do know*** *that one of my biggest strengths is establishing terrific relationships with my business leaders and clients. If I could turn that into a superpower, I'm confident that would enable me to do my job even better and deliver even better results for your organization."*

Then go on to give examples of how having the super-power of "establishing relationships" would help you do exactly that.

Example #2: Redirecting your response to emphasize some important knowledge you do have.

If you were asked: *"Tell me about your experience in using organizational change models to help managers implement change in their organizations?"* – and you have absolutely no practical experience using a change model, but do have knowledge about one, then you could speak to that as follows: ***"While I've not*** ***used a change model*** *in my work,* ***I am very familiar with the*** ***Kotter change model in theory*** *and here's how I would apply it..."*

Then you can elaborate more by describing how you would coach a manager through the model.

Example #3: Redirecting your comments to emphasize some related experience you have.

Let's say you applied for a Talent Acquisition position. And you're asked about your experience in using LinkedIn and other social media tools to attract job candidates. If you simply don't have this type of specialized experience and stumped, you can redirect your answer to a related area you do have experience with.

In this instance, you could highlight your experience in using job boards or contract recruiters and say, *"While my experience in utilizing social media is limited, I do have significant experience using innovative, non-traditional methods of recruiting job candidates – specifically job boards and contract recruiters -- that can be even MORE effective than social media in many cases. I feel very prepared to use these proven approaches to help you find the engineering candidates you need quickly – which I believe is your primary goal..."*

Example #4: Redirecting your answer to emphasize the research you've done.

Say you're applying for a position in HR that requires some previous experience in labor relations and are asked, *"What do you see as the risks in doing interest-based bargaining?"* — and you're totally clueless about that particular concept

Using the "redirection" approach, you might say something like: *"Interest-based bargaining is an area I'd need to research further. However, I have read extensively all about your past three Teamster labor settlements – especially as they relate to how you've outsourced work and used sub-contractors. And my research should provide a strong base of knowledge that will help me to quickly get up to speed on all of your labor strategies – including interest-based bargaining -- once I come aboard."*

In this case, your strength is all the research you've done... which you should leverage in your answer...even though you lack the knowledge about the specific question asked.

Some final points: When facing tough, weird and under-handed interview questions even if you have to create a somewhat awkward link between a question and the answer you'd like to give, it's always better to provide a "re-directed" answer, rather than no answer at all. This will allow you to keep your interview momentum going and demonstrate confidence and self-assurance to the interviewer.

Step #3:
As a last resort, if you still draw a blank, take the question as a homework assignment.

Let me be clear: I don't recommend doing this. But it's better than saying: "I don't know." This is the last resort. However, I'm a realist. If you're still completely and utterly stuck and nothing recommended so far helps you, then respond with: *"Nothing comes to mind at the moment. I'd like to do more research on it. May I have your card and follow up with you later today via an e-mail?"* Then be sure to keep your word and follow up with a well-thought-out response.

Obviously, this is NOT an ideal response. But it does demonstrate that even when you hit a roadblock, you don't give up. Some interviewers will appreciate your honesty and authenticity. Others will drop you immediately from further consideration if the question is a critical one and if it demonstrates that you don't fit the role. So again, only use this as a final, final, fall-back response.

Special Advice About Illegal Questions: What To Do When Interview Questions Cross The Line

Sometimes well-intentioned hiring managers ask illegal questions. Granted, if this person is a seasoned HR professional, he or she should know better, but everyone make mistakes. However, their error doesn't mean you should feel compelled to respond to anything they ask or if question asked makes you uncomfortable.

To handle illegal questions, I recommend that you establish your own personal boundaries and define which questions you WILL NOT answer – and do NOT go beyond them. For example, if the interviewer asks about your health. If that question is inside your boundaries, you might answer <u>directly</u> in an upbeat, confident manner by saying; *"I exercise daily, eat right, and according to the results of my last check-up, my health is excellent."* Keeping things light may also take some tension out the situation.

However, if the interviewer asks if you're married, and that's outside of your boundaries – rather than not answer the question, you can respond <u>indirectly</u> by saying… *"I'm in a solid relationship and thankful to have someone who supports me 100% in my career. If you're concerned that I won't be able to travel as much as I need to in order to provide HR support to all 15 sales regions throughout the country, I can assure you there won't be a problem. My last position required 60% overnight travel and I thrive on that sort of schedule…"*

This answer ("I'm in a solid relationship…") avoids a direct answer to the question. The next two sentences ("Some people may wonder…") address the underlying concern. And the last sentence ("My last position required…") accentuates a positive.

Of course, let me reiterate: you always, always, always have a choice not to answer an illegal question at all or flat-out tell the interviewer: *"That question is a personal one that I'd like to keep personal at this time."* But also know that making this statement might raise questions about what you're trying to hide and may spell the kiss of death for your candidacy. In this case my advice is: LIVE WITH IT!

When confronted with illegal questions, step back and think about what it means to you. Is the interviewer prying into your private life or did a legitimate question come out wrong with no ill intent meant? As an HR professional, trust your instincts and keep the answers in your comfort zone. As with any sticky interview situation, you want to remain calm and in control at all times.

The best advice is always to answer all questions the way <u>you want</u> to answer them – *directly, indirectly or not at all* -- get the offer and then decide whether you feel good about working for that organization.

Summary

It's impossible to anticipate every question. Expect to get stumped occasionally with questions that are strange, bizarre, illegal or that flat out leave you clueless.

When this happens, above all remain poised, professional, use the steps and tactics in this chapter and don't let them see you sweat. The more you treat the question and the interviewer with respect and show that you're genuinely concerned about addressing their needs – even if you have to "redirect" your response -- the better your outcome of your interview will be.

8

YOUR TURN! ASKING POWERFUL QUESTIONS THAT WILL WOW YOUR INTERVIEWERS

The end of the interview is your chance to ask powerful questions that will dazzle your interviewers. Most HR candidates use this time to ask wimpy questions and that's a huge mistake.

I knew a senior HR director who, at the end of his interview, asked: *"What strategies are you currently using to retain your high-potential marketing brand managers and sales people?"* He knew that the executive leadership team was struggling with this issue and this was also an area for which he had some significant experience.

His question resulted in a 90-minute HR strategy discussion. He won the job and was later told that particular question and the subsequent discussion were the reasons.

Now that's a great interview question!

If you're looking for an edge in your interviews, then ask terrific questions.

Here Are Examples of Weak Questions Along With Improved Ones:

Weak Question: In recruiting for your firm, what's most important in selecting new journalists?

Good Question: Given the dramatic changes in the newspaper industry, including the rapid shift to the online delivery of content, what are the new skills I'll be expected to look for in recruiting journalists for this company?

Weak Question: How does the new CEO feel about HR?
Good Question: With a new CEO and the publicized changes he's making in the company's product mix, what changes do you anticipate that he'll also be making in the direction of HR?

Weak Question: Are there morale issues among the employees I'll be supporting?
Good Question: I read online that the company has just announced plans to reorganize the West Coast operations. As a new HR director in the West Coast, how will this help the business and what impact will it have on the morale of the employees I'll be supporting?

Weak Question: What new services is the firm considering introducing in the marketplace?
Good Question: One of your strongest competitors, ABC Company has recently introduced the "Z" service. How does the company plan to compete with this brand new service innovation and maintain its competitive edge?

These are the types of questions that truly great HR candidates ask! They enable you to gather essential information about the company and the job...and they also convey that you've done your homework and that you're a strategic thinker who's interested in the company's success.

On The Other Hand, There Are Some Questions You Should Avoid

DON'T ask questions the interviewer can't answer. For example: *Congress is considering an increase in the minimum wage. If it passes, do you believe that the microeconomic im-*

pacts of the minimum wage will be offset by the macroeconomic effects driven by the last round of cuts to the Federal Reserve discount rate?

Huh? What the hell does that mean?

Want to make interviewers defensive and uncomfortable? Ask questions they don't know the answer to or can't answer because of confidentiality. This isn't a game show. There isn't a prize for stumping your interviewers or asking the cleverest question.

DON'T ask anything that you could have found out by doing a bit of independent research. That just makes you look lazy, unprepared and not ready for prime time.

DON'T pose great questions to the wrong people. Instead, customize your questions specifically to the roles of the individuals you're speaking with. For example, if you're fortunate enough to be talking with the CEO, ask about his or her long-term strategic vision for the company and how does he/she see HR fitting in. Find out about the biggest challenges as perceived from the highest office. These are all appropriate and fair game.

However, asking the CEO about medical insurance options is dumb. As is asking the human resources interviewer questions about the finer points of the company's emerging market merchandising strategy. Know who you're talking to and question them accordingly. With that in mind, here are....

12 Great Questions To Ask In Your Next Interview

Questions About The Position

#1: From what I've learned so far, the job is exactly what I'm looking for. But I'm curious, why is the position open? Is this a newly created role or are you seeking a replacement?

The answer to this question can give you all kinds of information you can't get anywhere else about the job. Was the last employee a poor performer? If so, what kind of things did that person fail to do? Maybe the last person was promoted. If so, find out what that person did that merited a move up. Their answers here reveal their expectations and reflect the company's values.

On the other hand, don't necessarily expect straight answers if the prior incumbent left under a cloud. If you suspect this is the case, then pose this question to a number of different people to see if you get a consistent story. It may be something or it may be nothing at all.

#2: Let's say for a moment that I am your candidate of choice. It is one year from today and you are conducting my performance review. What should I have demonstrated for you to say, "'I made a fantastic hire?"

This should tell you what your goals will be and how they will evaluate your performance. Here, of course, you are also subtly planting the idea that you are indeed a top performer and that you intend to be around for at least a year.

#3: What are results would you expect me to achieve during my first 3, 6, and 12 months of employment?

This is a more specific variation of question #2. Great HR candidates want to hit the ground running and know what the immediate priorities will be upfront.

The answer to this question will also give you tremendous insight into whether this job is a fit for you. If the position is a match and involves addressing some urgent HR issues, this allows you to say something along the lines of, *"My background in X makes me an ideal person to quickly address those challenges for you..."*

This question also will unearth hidden gems about how work gets done, who the role interacts with and the key job success factors that aren't clear from prior discussions or job descriptions.

#4: I've read through the position profile. However, beyond the written description, what does your ideal candidate really look like...and what are the common traits of your top performers in this role?

Hiring managers love this particular question because it's a signal to them that you care about being outstanding. And it's a fantastic way to get them to tell you exactly what they're looking for in an ideal candidate!

Ask this as early in the interview as you can manage. It will give you a strong idea of specifically what type of person the interviewer is looking to hire.

Once you know what the manager's hot buttons are, you'll be able to talk up and orient your experience towards their specific needs.

Questions For Your Business Leaders Or Clients

#5: I'm aware that your two biggest competitors are ABC and XYZ. What is it that they do that keeps you awake at night – and what things is the company doing to maintain its competitive edge?

There are many reasons why this question is powerful. First, it shows you've done your due diligence by demonstrating that you know the key players in the company's market. Secondly, it allows you to display your business acumen and your empathy for the business leader and the issues he or she is facing.

It's important that you don't limit your questions to just HR-related or people issues. As the HR pro, it's crucial that you express your interest in the business...and if you can, even go further and connect the dots between their business issues and how you can help address them as their HR business partner.

#6: What do you think of the quality of the HR services you've been receiving thus far? What would you like to see more of (or less of) from HR to help you run your business and be more successful?

This is one of the most valuable questions you can ask! You want to know how they feel about HR, what their expectations are…as well as what they're ready and not ready for. As they are ticking through their wish list, they're also giving you valuable insight into their agenda for you.

Even if you receive a hostile response from line manager about the quality of HR they're getting, take that as valuable information too. Their answer may reveal a difference you can make inside the company. Maybe they've never worked with a top-notch HR person before so they don't understand the value you can deliver. You need to know that in advance. Why? Because maybe you're at the stage in your career where you don't want the hassle of needing to prove the value of HR. On the other hand, maybe you are and welcome that challenge.

#7: I recently read in the Wall Street Journal where you are facing challenges regarding "X"? How do you plan to deal with X?

Every company faces any number of significant business challenges. "X" could be technological changes, new regulations, new competitors entering the market, rising prices, tough union negotiations…anything.

Doing the company research we discussed in Chapter 3 can pay off huge at this stage – and will give you a very clear picture of the company and a great foundation for asking this question.

Questions For Your Future Boss or Colleagues

#8: Describe the culture here and the qualities a person in this HR role needs to have in order to be successful in this environment?

It continues to surprise me that some HR candidates, especially those with extensive experience, don't ask about the corporate culture – or pick up on its nuances in the interview. Perhaps their egos are so big that they think they can get things done THEIR way, no matter what.

Don't make this mistake! It's crucial that you get your arms around the culture and then assess: "Do I fit?" And you can do this by picking up on the buzzwords used by your interviewers.

For example, some companies expect you to invest some time up front developing relationships, establishing trust, and learning how things get done. In these types of companies, cultural buzzwords like "collaborative," "teamwork," and "family-oriented culture" are used by just about everyone you meet. This could signal to you that if you come in like a "bull in a china shop" from day one, you risk alienating key supporters and gaining a negative reputation.

On the other hand, you have some employers who want you deliver results yesterday. Words like "result-driven," "hard charging," "type A personalities," and "entrepreneurial" are cues that this is the case. In this kind of culture, if you dilly dally taking too much time attempting to build friendships and learning the way things are done, you may be perceived as lazy, unfocused, and unproductive.

This question enables you to probe for clues about the culture and to self-assess your personal fit with it.

#9: Describe your management style. I understand the company does 360 surveys. Would you mind sharing highlights of your most recent results and how others regard you as a manager?

This is a ballsy, but crucial question to pose to your boss. And it's another question of cultural fit – specifically, will you mesh with the management style of your new boss? His or her management style will have a dramatic impact on the majority of your waking hours if you take this job. How do they interact with the team? How do they delegate? How do they react to mistakes? Listen carefully to their answers – and to what they do NOT say. You'll want to further probe the latter.

#10: What drew you to this company?

This simple, but powerful question can be asked to ANY of your interviewers. It helps establish an immediate personal bond between you and them. Everyone's favorite topic is him/herself. This question leads to additional ones such as: *"What has been your path to this position?"* or *"What do you enjoy most about working here?"*

This also allows you to uncover perks about the job you might not have heard about otherwise. Maybe there's a gym or great childcare or profit-sharing. Maybe the culture is very collaborative, rather than competitive. Maybe they're really strong at talent development and grooming people for their next step up.

#11: Why would someone want to work for your organization instead of your competitor – and why would they choose stay?

Only ask this if you believe you're a top HR contender for the job. You are giving them an opportunity to sell you on the position and to give you some ideas about whether the job would be right for you. If they sell you hard, it's also an indicator of how strong a candidate you truly are.

#12: You mentioned earlier having been here for ___ years. As you look ahead, what excites you personally about the future here in this department?"

This question, regardless of the answer, will allow you to gauge the passion of the interviewer – and objectively assess the potential of the position available. *This is especially helpful to ask of those who have been with the organization for some time – and have seen it go through various ups and downs.* If the interviewer looks down at the desk, or chooses their words too carefully, they may be indirectly communicating that you're going to be taking on a massive, maybe impossible challenge in this particular firm.

If, on the other hand, they sit back in their chair, eyes lit up with a sincere smile stretching across their face, you may be able to assume the interviewer sees real potential in the company and in the job.

However, if they don't answer at all, citing "corporate policy," that tells you quite a bit about the company also (and may be an indication that your best course of action is to run away).

Summary

Asking great questions like the examples in this chapter positions you as an excellent candidate. Overall, your questions should provide you with a penetrating insight into the following:

- The top three to five critical job requirements
- How success is measured on the job
- The top job priorities in the next three, six, and twelve months
- Your greatest challenges to performing the job well
- Any doubts or hesitations the hiring manager has about hiring you
- The company's culture, financial strength and stability
- The hiring manager's management style
- The type of HR person most successful at this company
- The company's top two or three challenges
- What keeps the hiring manager up at night and problems that are nagging him/her
- How the hiring manager got to her position
- Whether this position is new or if you will be replacing a person who has moved on
- Details about the selection process (steps, timeframe, number of candidates, whether there is an inside candidate, and so on)
- How and when to follow up after your interview

This list isn't exhaustive, but is simply a representative sample of what you should know when your interviews conclude. It might seem like a lengthy list, but it really isn't.

Some of these questions might get answered without you even asking. Some you'll be able to ask to specific interviewers during the flow of the conversation. You can also space these out and decide which ones are most appropriate for the first, second or your later interviews.

And, of course, some you'll have loaded and ready to go when the interview is drawing to a close and you're asked: "Do you have any questions for us?"

Onward!

9

THE MOST IMPORTANT QUESTION
TO ASK AT THE END OF YOUR INTERVIEW

Of all the questions you can possibly ask, there is one that's crucial and should be saved for the end of your interview. It's the **"Concerns Question"** and it should be posed as follows:

"One last question: I know you're interviewing other candidates, but I'd like your insight. Do you have any <u>concerns</u> at all about me as a top candidate for the position?

Other ways of asking this are as follows:
- *Do you have any reservations about me as a candidate for this position?*
- *Based on what we've talked about today, how well do I fit the ideal profile of the person you're looking for?*
- *Is there any reason you wouldn't recommend moving me forward in the selection process as a top candidate?*

However you phrase it…ASK IT!…and view any response you get as a "concern" that must be addressed.

Yes, this is a gutsy question. Yes, it takes a lot of confidence open yourself up for feedback so early in the selection process.

But you have to do it. You'll shortchange yourself if you don't. While this may feel pretty bold and pushy, this type of assertiveness in interviews is what gets people hired.

Why Is This Question So Important?

When you get an answer to the "Concerns Question," it mitigates one of the most uncomfortable parts of the job-search process...waiting for the hiring manager to call after an interview. Because their answer will potentially reveal any doubts or reservations they have about offering you the job. That's why it's so powerful.

Here's How To Address Their Doubts, Objections Or Potential Concerns About You As A Candidate

If their concerns seem vague or general...

For example, if they say: "Your greatest challenge will be building relationships with all your clients quickly. They all travel quite a bit, keep packed schedules and are tough to catch up with."

Well, frankly, that's a generic concern. Any candidate will face that same challenge. And it doesn't reveal any objections the interviewer may have about you specifically. So, in this case, you should probe further by asking: *"Is there anything about my background and skills **in particular** that suggests that this would be a more difficult task for me than for other candidates?"* This is a gentle way of suggesting that the answer is not specific enough. And now that you've opened up this line of discussion, you can dig even deeper by asking, *"Can you think of any other concerns related specifically to my background and skills?"*

If no concerns are mentioned...

If the hiring authority states that there are no concerns or only minor (but manageable) ones, it can be an indication that you did well in the interview and you are under consideration for the position.

However, it can also mean that the interviewer isn't ready to reveal this to you at this stage and that's fine too -- no news is good news at this juncture. But, if you sense that's not the case, you can calmly ask: *"Is there any other information I can provide you to support my candidacy?"*

If a concern emerges that hasn't been discussed...

For example, if the interviewer says, "My biggest concern is that you don't seem to have the amount of HR leadership experience we'd ideally like."

You now have an opportunity to correct this perception you're now hearing for the first time by replying: *"I'm so glad you brought that up. We didn't have a chance to discuss my experience leading the HR task force to improve employee engagement at our Atlanta manufacturing facility. It really highlights my leadership. Let me tell you about it..."*

If the concern mentioned can be overcome...

The interviewer might express a concern that you've addressed before – perhaps in a previous job. If so, use that job experience as an example to illustrate how you will overcome that concern in this job.

For example: *"You are correct that I'm not very experienced in leading a multi-functional HR team. However, I've overcome similar "experience" challenges before. When I started my previous job in Organization Development, I wasn't experienced at facilitating executive strategy meetings with powerful personalities either.*

However, immediately after being hired, I took a two-day course in group facilitation, got coached by the best executive group facilitator in the company and got regular feedback. Within four weeks, I was facilitating executive sessions with terrific feedback. Once hired, I would put this same dedicated focus on learning to build my experience in leading the multi-functional HR team here..."

If you haven't addressed a similar concern before, then lay out a game plan for how you'd propose addressing the concern and ask the interviewer whether she thinks your plan is viable.

If the concern mentioned is a misconception...

One of my former colleagues was interviewing for a position as the VP of Compensation and Benefits. She had a strong background in implementing state-of-the-art compensation systems and spoke extensively about this experience. At the end of the interview, she asked the "Concerns Question."

The CHRO responded by saying, "Our compensation systems are old and out-of-date. You're a real pro at comp. Frankly, I'm concerned that you'll want to implement a brand new compensation system right away...and we cannot afford that at this time or take the organization through this kind of massive change."

My former colleague wasted no time and immediately addressed the CHRO's misconception: *"Thanks for sharing that. You should know that I wouldn't dare just implement a new system. Every organization is different. I first would evaluate the system you have here, assess the readiness of the organization and see whether it can be upgraded in small stages with minimal impact on the business and within the company's budget. I would then work with you and the rest of the leadership team on a longer-term strategic plan to prioritize and make changes at a pace that's comfortable and affordable for the organization...."* Her answer satisfied the CHRO, and she got the job.

Had she not asked the "Concerns Question" directly after the interview, the CHRO would've said to the rest of the interview team, "This woman's not a fit. She just wants to spend our money on expensive new systems..."

Interviews can lead to many misconceptions that can go unaddressed. Smoke them out and deal with them on the spot.

Summary

Addressing the interviewer's fears, uncertainties and concerns about hiring you is one of the primary goals in your interview. A great way to surface those early in the selection process is by asking the "Concerns Question" at the end of your interview. And then leaning into what you hear.

Directly addressing interviewer concerns and doubts conveys confidence, gives you an opportunity to sell yourself and adds more credibility to your candidacy.

10

CLOSE YOUR INTERVIEW WITH POISE & CONFIDENCE

Once you've asked your questions and completed your round of interviews, it's time to close and requires that you:
1. Ask for the job.
2. Thank them for their time.
3. Clarify the next steps.

#1: Ask for the job

This is one thing many HR interviewees fail to do. If you are really interested in the position say so. Crank up the energy in your voice and offer one (or a combination) of these closing statements (provided they are true for you):

- *I have a great understanding of the organization and the position. Thank you. With my experience in___ I feel that I could quickly and value to the organization and am very excited about the possibility of working here.*

- *I'd like you to know that I'm extremely interested this position. Although I'm looking at another opportunity right now, this position with your organization is at the top of my list and where I could make the biggest contribution."* (Note: Make sure you can state this truthfully. Your "other opportunity" could simply be remaining in your current position. You won't, of course, disclose this other opportunity to the interviewer!)

#2: Thank each interviewer for their time.

A simple and sincere *"Thank you for your time and all the information, Jennifer"* will suffice (making sure you use the interviewer's name). If there was something that came up in the interview, follow up with a promise to send an article or brochure. *"I will not forget to forward that article we discussed from HR Magazine."*

And, with that, your interview is done. Congratulations! Making it through the interview process is something to be proud of and is a great learning experience, even if you aren't offered the job.

#3: Before leaving, clarify what the next steps will be.

When you finish your round of interviews, make sure you close with the primary hiring authority and/or recruiter by stating: *"I'd really like to work for your organization and believe this is a great fit for me. What should I anticipate the next step being?"*

It's a nice, open-ended question and you deserve to know what to expect. After all, you're a busy person, and you gave them your time as much as they gave you theirs.

You'll probably hear a response such as, "We have several other candidates to talk to. Once we go through that process, you should be hearing back from us."

Unfortunately, this is a typical answer is much too vague. In response, request specifics: *"Great. Is there an anticipated*

timeframe for that?" However, keep it soft, light and non-stressful. Then clarify: *"That's great. If I don't hear from you by Wednesday, should I call you?"* If you haven't heard from the hiring manager by the following Wednesday, you can place a call and say: *"As you suggested, I'm calling to follow up on our interview from last week."* This obligates the hiring manager to respond.

After making such a closing statement, the rest remains pretty much up to the hiring manager and the employer. That's not to say, however, that you've done all you can to ultimately become the chosen candidate.

In the next few chapters, we'll cover the sending timely "Thank You" notes and other appropriate follow-up steps.

11

THANK YOU NOTES:
THE TWO TYPES YOU NEED & HOW
TO CRANK THEM OUT LIGHTNING FAST!

In my experience, an alarming number of HR job candidates don't bother sending thank you notes after interviews. And they are making a big mistake! A recent *CareerBuilder* survey showed that 22% of employers are less likely to hire a candidate who does not send a thank you. And 91% like being thanked, according to the same survey.

So there's no downside, just upside in doing it – and it benefits you in a variety of ways. Thank you notes strengthen the impression you left after the interview. They convey your interest in the position. And they can make you memorable and stand out from your competitors.

So it's definitely in your best interest to send them.

However, it can be time-consuming pain in the butt to write to every single person with whom you interviewed. So let me give you a simple 3-point formula that will help you quickly compose them. This formula consists of the following:

1. Thank the person.
2. Mention something you liked about the interview.
3. Restate your interest in the job.

Let's each of these down point by point:

#1: In the first sentence, thank the person for meeting with you.

- If you liked them, or if they were particularly warm and friendly, you can say something like *"Thank you for making my interview today so pleasant."*
- If they were more straightforward and businesslike, you can write, *"Thank you for taking the time to meet with me today."*

#2: Then mention something that you especially liked about the interview.

- If they were personal or friendly, say something personal, such as, *"I particularly enjoyed our talk about [whatever you—and they—connected on or specifically enjoyed talking about]."*
- If they were more businesslike, you should be more businesslike and write, *"I was glad to learn more about _____ (whatever you and they discussed about the business or the position that stood out in your mind)."*

#3: Finally, restate your interest in the position.

- **Warm and Friendly version:** *"I would be thrilled to work for [name of company], and hope to meet you again as a colleague."*
- **Straightforward and Business version:** *"I am now even more interested in working with [name of organization], and appreciate your help with the process."*

Here are some examples of what this looks like when you put all three points together:

The Warm & Friendlier Version:

June 2, 20xx

Dear Judy,

Thank you for making my interview today so warm and pleasant. I particularly enjoyed our talk about the teamwork and collaboration that occurs when Recruiting & Staffing teams are challenged to recruit tough-to-fill positions.

The energy and excitement that you conveyed sounds exactly like the kind of culture I'd like to be a part of. I would be thrilled to work in the Talent Acquisition department for the Netflix organization and hope to meet you again soon as a colleague.

Sincerely,
John Smith

The Straightforward & More Businesslike Version:

June 2, 20xx,

Dear Bryan,

Thank you for your time in meeting with me today. I was happy to learn more about your take on the role HR has played in using social media to recruit passive job candidates. It's clearly impressive and a competitive edge for the business.

I am now even more interested in joining the Talent Acquisition department for the Netflix organization and appreciate your help with the process.

Sincerely,
John Smith

Some Additional Key Points:

Use both email and snail mail.

Send an emailed note immediately after the interview and then send a typed letter the next day via "snail mail." There's nothing wrong with saying "thank you" twice.

However, you should get both done within 24 hours to ensure you are still fresh in your interviewer's mind. Also, you'll want to ensure that your 1 or 2 brief, positive comments aren't worded exactly in the same way in both notes.

Keep letters short!

Because email is often read on smart phones, keep your note concise. And, though your snail-mailed letter can be a bit longer, it doesn't give you license to ramble. Keep it to no more than 2 to 3 brief paragraphs and one page max (a half page is ideal).

It's fine to insert one paragraph in the note to clarify some point you didn't articulate as well as you would have liked. For example, *"You asked about my past successes in managing HR vendors and I forget to mention the XYZ vendor who provides payroll services for over 2,000 employees in my current organization. Under my direction, they lowered our costs by 11% and their execution has been flawless."* But again, make this additional paragraph as brief as possible. Resist the temptation to oversell yourself – this note won't completely override your performance in the interview, it will just supplement it.

Don't use the identical letter for everyone.

Personalize your letters. It's fine for each one to have similar opening and closing statements as long as a majority of the note is different and is customized with details from your talks with each specific interviewer. You never know who really influences the decision to hire you.

Finally, don't suck up to the senior people.

Resist the urge to send thank you notes to only the most senior people you interviewed with. You could do yourself damage if you're perceived to be kissing up to the wrong person or excluding those whose input is considered valuable. So don't take that risk, *thank everyone who interviewed you.*

Summary

All it takes is a few minutes to follow this simple 3-point formula for your thank you notes. After that, make sure they are personalized and sent by both snail mail and email and you've got this nailed. Lightning fast!

12

SECOND ROUND INTERVIEWS: HOW TO PREPARE FOR & EXCEL AT THEM

Second (and even third, fourth and fifth) round interviews are common in HR. Typically, the higher up on the food chain your target position is, the more rounds of interviews you can expect.

But make no mistake about it, being asked to come in for a second interview is definitely great news. Yes, it can be a pain in the butt if you're already holding down a full-time gig, but there are many valid reasons why they want you to return:

- You may need to speak with the HR higher-ups for final approval before they make you an offer.
- They may want you to chat with other members of the team to determine if you'll work well with them.
- Perhaps the role has dramatically changed (e.g. they've decided to consolidate two HR jobs into one to save money, or it now reports to a different manager, etc.).
- Or it may be down to just you and a couple of other finalists, and they're trying to decide which of you will be the best fit for the role.
- Or maybe the last person in the job was so horrible they're taking extra steps to ensure they don't screw things up again.

Whatever their reasons are, be patient with the process because making a return visit can provide additional benefits to you too. To illustrate, let me share a personal story…

Years ago, I responded to an ad in the Chicago Tribune for a Human Resources position at the Quaker Oats Company.

Not to be cocky, but from the ad, I knew that I had the perfect background for this job. I could tell from its brief description that the culture was fast-paced and the position had high-impact, which was right up my alley.

The call came several days after I applied. I was ecstatic and looked forward to coming in. I was told the appropriate dress was "everyday business attire" (shirt and tie), much different than today. So I went to a local men's store and bought a new suit for the occasion. I was ready to play the interviewing game.

The first interview went perfectly. I connected well with the director of Human Resources, my potential new boss, and I was certain this was going to be my new job. However, before I had a chance to celebrate, he told me that I needed to come back to see the divisional vice president of Human Resources.

I aced that interview too. Our personalities just clicked. Again, I believed the job was mine. But one more time my euphoria was put on hold when I was asked to return once again -- this time to meet with the director of Human Resources Development and four other HR directors and managers.

Following those meetings, believe it or not, I was scheduled yet again a week later to meet the three key business leaders that I would be supporting in this newly created HR role.

To make a long story short, I ended up coming back for a total of 5 interviews on 5 different days. That meant 5 days of sneaking away early from work; 5 trips of 45 miles each in my car driving to and from those interviews; 5 different suits; and 5 days of being at the top of my game.

I never complained.

Eventually, I landed the job and enjoyed a long, satisfying career at Quaker Oats...and I've never had any regrets.

Looking back, I realized that putting me through those steps was actually beneficial for both the company and me.

- By the time I joined Quaker, I knew that four of the key individuals I met with (including my new boss) were going to determine my future success in the organization. Meeting them early as part of the interview process enabled them to get to know me, buy-in and support my hire.
- Finally, through discussions I had with these four people, I had gained an intimate knowledge of what each of their goals were -- which meant that before I started, I knew what *my* goals needed to be in order to be successful in their eyes. This reduced my day one anxiety and enabled me to hit the ground running in my new role.

The point: Multiple rounds of interviews can be an agonizing pain in the butt, but they are essential in providing an important launching pad for your career with your new employer. .

So take second interviews seriously. Be patient with the process and prepare for them as thoroughly as you did for your first round interviews...if not more so!

How Should You Get Ready For Second Interviews?

#1: Step up your planning and preparation.

Begin by asking if there is anything you should bring with you to the second round. This could be anything from (non-confidential) samples of HR projects you've completed to recommendation letters from prior employers.

Also request any additional materials that can provide more insight about the organization. It could be a copy of the HR strategy, their key priorities and organization charts.

If you dressed in business attire (suit and tie for men; jacket, blouse, skirt and heels for women) for the first interview, do so again, even if everyone at the office wore shorts. The only exception is if they say to you, "Please feel free to dress casually."

Even with that said, casual means clothes that are neat, laundered and ironed. It's very likely you'll be meeting some higher-ups this time around, so you want to dress to impress them.

#2: Review your first round of interviews.

Go through all your notes and all the previous homework you did on the organization and every person you spoke with at your first interview.

Analyze the points you made about your skills and experience during those meetings and identify as best you can what your interviewers found impressive, as well as what they found questionable.

You'll want to attack the second round with confidence by giving them more of what they liked and provide stronger answers for any questions you struggled with.

#3: Know your interviewers.

Before your second interviews, you'll likely be provided a schedule identifying who you'll be talking to. They'll be different people so research them on LinkedIn and Google just as you did your first set of interviewers.

You want to know how long they've been with the company, what titles they have held, what companies they worked for previously and what schools they attended. Look for a shared interest you can casually use to break the ice.

#4: Have a 60-day plan.

You established during your first-round interviews that you have the skills to do the job. During the second round you want to position yourself as the number one candidate.

One of the most effective ways to do this is to provide the employer with a 60-day plan. This doesn't have to be in writing but you should be prepared to talk through your game plan for getting up to speed and providing results within a few months.

If it comes down to you versus a couple of other strong candidates, articulating such a specific plan for making a immediate impact that can help elevate you from the pack.

#5: Ask deeper questions.

Take the time to prepare a list of any questions about the company that went unanswered (or unasked) in the first round. You'll want to probe deeper and ask more detailed questions in this round of the process. Revisit the questions in Chapter 8 if you need additional help. You should walk in with at least two to three questions for each person on your schedule.

For example, if your original interviewer is part of the second interview process, you'll definitely want to ask her:

- *Has the definition of this position changed since the last time we spoke?*
- *Do you have any new questions or emerging concerns I can address?*
- *What kind of timetable are you working on at this point?*

Likewise, if you are introduced to potential colleagues, you'll want to ask them:

- *What do you like best about working here? Least?*
- *What's a typical workday like?*
- *What kind of promotion potential is there?*

#6: Tips for handling group/panel interviews.

Panel interviews are increasingly being used for HR candidates in second round interviews. Here, a group of people meet with you simultaneously and take turns asking you a series of questions tag-team style.

This kind of interview helps them assess how you interact with others, many of whom may be your managers, clients and colleagues. It's common for the hiring manager, an HR representative, someone from upper management, and a potential peer to be present.

The content of this interview and your answers will not be any different than they would be with a single interviewer, but your greeting, eye contact and other dynamics will change a little. So, just in case you're set up to interview with a panel, you can't go wrong following these tips.

- **Ask the person setting up your interview, *"Who will I be interviewing with and what are their titles?"*** You should request basic bios on each of the panel members in advance – and then, of course, check them out yourself on LinkedIn or by Googling them.

- **As mentioned previously, prepare as thoroughly as you did for your one-on-one interview, and then some.** Memorize your resume – you want answers on the tip of your tongue. Study the job description to understand what the interviewers are looking for. Assemble some friends who are familiar with panel interviewing and brainstorm questions or have a have mock panel interview. If you have time, video record this session so you can see what you can improve.

- **Relax, focus, and breathe! When you enter the room, shake hands with each person on the panel.** It's fantastic if you can remember everyone's name, but that's not always possible. You don't have to address each person by name, nor do you have to introduce yourself by first and last names to all of them. A handshake, with direct eye contact, a smile, and a simple *"Hello"* or *"Good morning"* will do.

- **Treat the panel interview like a business meeting and ask if it is okay to take notes.** Jotting notes will also help you remember important points (and names) and occasionally buy you a few extra moments when responding to tough, probing questions.

- **Position your chair somewhere that allows you to keep all the interviewers in your line of sight.** Don't be afraid to physically move your chair, You can simply say *"I'd like to be able to see everyone, so I'm just going to move my chair over here."* It's unlikely that anyone will object. On the contrary, they'll note your initiative as a positive trait.

- **Be prepared for different questions from different peer interviewers.** Typically, each person is assigned a unique role. For example, one may be there to ask questions which assess your related HR experience; another may be there to probe into your leadership and teamwork skills with behavioral-based questions (see Chapter 6); and still another may be assigned to assess how well you're able to manage the overall meeting.

- **Take it one question at a time, one person at a time.** Direct your answer primarily to the individual asking the question, while also making eye contact with the rest of the panel.

- **Look for the key decision-maker on the panel.** He or she is often the person who is last to the meeting because of a busy schedule, or the person to whom all the other heads turn when there is a question or when you respond.

- **If anyone on the panel seems hellbent on disagreeing with everything you say, don't take it personally.** He could be having a bad day (or a bad life). He could testing you to see if you have the courage to stick to your guns or whether you have what it takes to make it in a high-pressure HR position. Above all stay calm and professional if you get tough questions or disapproving looks. Repeat your answers if they seem misunderstood. Smile. Go with the flow. If you're feeling especially pressured, then take a "time out" to excuse yourself for a restroom break – and then take some deep breaths and collect yourself while alone. But try not to resort to this tactic unless it's absolutely necessary. You don't want the panel to feel that you crack under stress...after all, what will you do when a major HR project is on the line and a client throws you an unexpected curve ball?

- **When the floor is opened up for you to ask questions, address at least one question to each person on the panel.** When the session ends, a simple and sincere *"Thank you for the opportunity to visit with all of you today"* will suffice and be sure to shake each person's hand before leaving.

Closing The Deal
With Second-Round Interviews

Just as you did in the first round, when the second round of interviews conclude, you'll want to speak to the hiring authority or decision-maker separately to **make it clear that you're interested in the position** (if you are). This needs to be done professionally and with confidence (refer to the talking points in Chapter 10 to guide you). Additionally:

- **If you're not given an immediate verbal job offer or a commitment, ask him or her to define the decision-making timeline.** Try to nail down a specific date when the final hiring decision will be made.

- **Send thank you notes to everyone you spoke with.** As mentioned previously, it's not okay to let this slide, unless you're 100% certain you don't want the job. However, if you met with an entire department consisting of 30 people, you don't have to write individual e-mails to everyone there. You can pick someone you connected with and ask him to forward your e-mail to the rest of the team. Follow the tips in Chapter 11 when composing your notes.

- **Wait three to five days after your second interview, and then call the hiring decision-maker to check in.** Revisit the timeline that was previously communicated: has it changed? When should you call again? See if there are any new issues you can address. If you're part of the process, you're poised to become the solution.

- **Don't be an annoying pest, but do stay in touch.** Make it part of your routine to call your contact within the company at least once a week for an update. Make sure that deadline doesn't pass without your receiving the employer's full consideration. If the deadline passes and you're certain no one has been chosen for the position, don't become discouraged. At some point they may tell you that hiring position is on hold or being postponed. If that's the case, ask them frankly when they believe the process will move forward. Depending on their answer, continue to stay in touch (though perhaps not so frequently) in order to stay in the loop and avoid getting passed over.

Summary

Second (and even third, fourth and fifth) round interviews are common in HR. Clearly, you've done something right if you're being asked to return after the first interview. To ace your second visit, be sure to step up your preparation, know your interviewers, prepare a 60-day plan and be ready to nail panel/group interviews (if they're required). Above all, don't forget to close the deal.

.

13

12 STRATEGIES FOR NEGOTIATING YOUR JOB OFFER & GETTING THE BEST POSSIBLE PAY PACKAGE

Congratulations! You've got the job offer. This means the employer has now switched from "shopper" to "buyer" and the salary dance has fully begun.

Make no mistake about it, most employers will expect you to negotiate. For that reason, their initial offer will be "competitive," but it will seldom be their "absolute best and final" offer. With this in mind, you won't offend anyone by asking for more, provided you do so in a constructive, respectful and professional manner.

To help you, in this chapter, we'll cover 12 strategies for negotiating the best possible pay package. So let's begin.

Strategy #1:
If You're Extended The Job Offer Verbally, Respond With A "Moment of Silence"

Many employers extend job offers verbally first, either by phone or in person. And if this happens, be careful!

It's tempting to jump right in and start babbling about how excited you are about the offer. But it's better to keep your cool. No matter what the number is, whether it's high or low, your first response should be to: (a) thank them for the offer, (b) pause and then (c) repeat the number thoughtfully and nonjudgmentally – as follows:

> *"Thank you very much for the offer. So the base salary for the position is $125,000. Hmmm…"*

Then stop talking. This is called the "Moment of Silence." Let the employer make the next move. During your silence, know that the employer doesn't want to piss you off and does not want to lose you either. They've invested a lot of their time in the interview process and they want to reel you in.

So, if you restrain yourself and don't bite on the initial offer immediately, there's a possibility they might increase it on the spot – especially if they're pressured to fill the job. If they do, just like that you've just got an instant raise! This is ideally what you want to occur and is the primary purpose of staying silent.

However, ninety-five percent of the time, this ain't gonna happen! Realistically, if you're talking to a very experienced and savvy recruiter, he or she may choose to just wait out your silence and say nothing. Or they will take note of your hesitancy and ask for your feedback or if you'd like to accept the offer.

In any of these cases, it's your turn to make the next move.

Strategy #2:
Get the Offer in Writing
So You Can Buy Some Time
To Think It Over

Your next response should be:

> *"Sarah, again thanks so much for the offer. I'd like some time to consider it. I look forward to getting the details of the offer*

in writing. I'll then call you back within 24 hours after I receive it to discuss any questions I have. Will that work for you?"

Don't commit or accept anything yet! If you can, always get everything in writing upfront. If the employer refuses to give you time to think about the offer or doesn't want to put the offer in writing until you accept it...then run, don't walk, to the nearest exit. Fortunately, most employers are not crazy, and they know full well that they need to give you a formal, written offer and adequate time to consider it.

Do the same for offers made by phone. Simply ask the employer to e-mail or express mail the details of the written offer to you or arrange to pick it up.

Aim for at least three to five days to consider an offer. Some employers may respond by with, "This offer is good for 48 hours," or "We really need a response by Friday morning." If that's not enough time for you, ask for more. If you ask for a two months, you won't get it. But it's perfectly reasonable to say:

"Look, I appreciate that you want to move forward quickly, and I do, too. But my spouse is out of town until Thursday, so I really can't get back to you before Monday".

Or you might say: *"I try to avoid making important decisions in a rush. I'd really like to have three days to consider your offer. Is that all right?"*

Most employers will don't want to appear unreasonable and your request will usually be granted. Obviously, if you make your decision early, you can give it to them before your deadline. But if you do need the extra time, this gives it to you.

But what if the employer persists in trying to extract a commitment from you in advance? For example, if he says:

"We'd really like to have you on board with our HR team immediately. Could you start in two weeks?"

Simply stick to your guns and respond with:

> *"Thank you. I appreciate all the time you've spent with me and I thoroughly enjoyed meeting with the HR team. However, I would like to review the complete written offer package first before I'm in a position to make any commitments."*

Rarely, but sometimes, you'll have a super-aggressive employer who will want to press the issue even further:

> *"Well, yes, we'll do all that official paperwork later. But will you be coming to work for us? We'd like to know."*

You need to stay pleasant but firm. Blame a spouse or significant other:

> *"You know, if I made a decision like this without talking to my [wife/husband/fiancé/significant other], I wouldn't have a place to live anymore. I want to show him (or her) something in writing."*

Or you can again reiterate that such an important decision deserves careful consideration:

> *"I really need a few days to think about this. Making a job change isn't something I take lightly, and I'd like to make sure I give your offer the proper thought and consideration.."*

Again, don't get sucked into saying "Yes," or committing to anything until you have the formal written job offer in hand. This will give you the maximum possible negotiating leverage.

Strategy #3:
Acknowledge Your Receipt Of The Written Offer Right Away

When the offer arrives in writing, immediately reply (e-mail, voicemail or text) with a short message thanking the employer for the offer and indicating that you will consider it and return a reply within the agreed-upon time frame. Again, if the employer indicates that you must respond within less time than you feel comfortable with, simply say:

"Thank you for the offer package you sent via FedEx this morning. You indicated that you would like a response by the end of this week, but I'd really like to take the weekend to think it over and give your offer the consideration it deserves. Would it be all right if I called you on Monday morning?"

As mentioned before, refusing your request puts the employer in an awkward position, so you probably don't have anything to worry about.

Strategy #4:
Evaluate The Offer Carefully And Pinpoint Those Items You Want To Negotiate

In reviewing the written offer, make sure it reflects everything mentioned verbally. However, don't get stuck on salary alone. Evaluate the whole package! Maybe you're getting stock options and wonderful health benefits. Think through the value of what these are worth to you.

Then make a list of the <u>top two or three most important, "must have" items</u> you'd like to negotiate. You'll create problems if your list is too long. Below is a list of some of the typical items to consider negotiating as part of your total compensation package.

- Base salary
- Sign-on bonus
- Timing of your first salary review
- Annual performance bonus (amount and eligibility criteria)
- Guaranteed minimum annual performance bonus (at least in the first year)

- Weeks of vacation
- Relocation cost reimbursement, short-term housing
- Buying your home (or covering the cost of your home sale)
- Loan to purchase home
- Tuition reimbursement
- Stock options
- Restricted stock grants
- Discounted stock purchases
- Reimbursement for home office expenses (e.g. internet services)
- Company car and/or mileage reimbursements
- Laptop computer, tablet
- Mobile cell phone
- Special leadership training or conferences
- Payment of professional membership dues
- Paid subscriptions to *HR Magazine, HR Executive* or other HR-related business journals
- Pension and/or 401(k) (generally available to all full-time employees and not negotiable. Pensions are rare these days.)
- Health benefits (Some aspects are covered by benefit plans, but others may be negotiable or available as payments in lieu of the actual benefits.)
- Deferred compensation
- Profit sharing
- Financial, tax, and/or estate planning services
- Legal planning services
- School tuition for children
- Subsidized and/or financial assistance for day care
- Potential forgiveness of loans based on agreed-to criteria (tenure and/or performance)
- Gym membership
- First- or business-class air travel (on very long flights)
- Flexible work schedules or work-from-home
- Tax gross-ups for taxable benefits
- Severance pay and termination provisions
- Career assistance for spouse or partner

After you've put together the "shopping list" of what you want to negotiate, then contact the hiring authority and set up a time to discuss the package in person. Don't ask for a meeting to talk about *"compensation."* Instead, ask to get together to *"answer a few final questions"* to help you in making your decision.

<u>Important Point:</u> **Don't attempt to negotiate by e-mail.**

An in-person meeting, where you can read the other person's non-verbals, is the most productive setting and gives you best chance of getting what you want. Obviously, if you are living in a different city, you might not be able to conduct this meeting in person, and in that case opt for a phone meeting.

At the end of every phone conversation, be sure you recap what was agreed-to in writing (e-mail is fine) as confirmation. You don't want to leave room for error. Misunderstandings can cause hard feelings and jeopardize the job offer or your future working relationship.

But don't be greedy. Remember: it's not mandatory that you negotiate! If you've reviewed the written offer – and the scope of the position, salary, bonus, benefits, perks are attractive and is a perfect match for your needs and expectations – then call the employer back, thank them for the offer and accept it! And move forward with your life.

On the other hand, if you're looking to maximize your offer, it's time to move on to…

Strategy #5:
Negotiate & Get Agreement On The Cash Compensation Elements First (Salary, Bonuses, Stock, Equity, etc)

Obviously, there are many components that comprise your total compensation package that you will want to understand along with the few you'll want to upgrade.

However, before discussing these items, I recommend that you begin *first* by negotiating and getting agreement on your cash compensation elements (e.g. salary, bonuses, stock, equity, etc.).

When the time comes, here's how to start that discussion:

1: Express appreciation for the offer:

"John, I want to thank you again for the offer. I'm flattered that you think I'm the right person for the job and I'm excited about the challenge it offers."

2: Clarify the job parameters.

"Let me first ensure we both have the same understanding about the position. This would be a full-time, exempt position as director of Human Resources for your Emerging Foods Division. I would be reporting to the divisional vice-president of Human Resources and also report on a strong dotted-line basis to the General Manager of Emerging Foods.

I'd be responsible for a staff of 3 HR managers. I would be expected to lead and manage all HR programs, employee relations and talent development initiatives for the division. I'd also be expected to lead some aggressive recruiting and talent acquisition initiatives to staff up the division by 10 percent over the next year.

Do I have that straight?"

Be sure you have accurately summarized the position. Wait for the hiring authority to agree or clear up any differences before you proceed.

3: Then make your counter-offer and state your case for an increase in cash compensation, based on the value you can bring to the position.

One way to do this is to sell your ability to solve the employer's most pressing problem (that you uncovered during the interview process) as the rationale for your counter-offer.

"I'm fine with the 25% bonus you've offered. However, I believe with my track record of results, a starting salary of $135,000 would be more appropriate.

And here's my thinking on this: My experience with ABC Corp will enable me to hit the ground running on day one, successfully lead the HR team and deliver on your #1 objective, which is to staff up the division by 10% in the first year.

With that in mind, what can you do in $135,000 range?"

You've now counter-offered their original offer of $125,000 and laid your number on the table. Make sure that number is not your "last and final number" but gives you some flexibility to come down. You might typically target your counter-offer at 5-10% above their initial offer.

In the above example, if you're ultimately willing to accept $130,000, starting at $135,000 is far from outlandish and gives you (and the employer) some room for compromise.

Strategy #6:
Effectively Address The Employer's Response To Your Counter-Offer Diplomatically But Assertively

Now that you've counter-offered, it's now the employer's move. As they respond, avoid being confrontational and don't react in an insulted or scornful manner. Such an attitude will only harm or even sabotage your negotiation. And even if you don't lose the offer, you'll potentially damage your relationship with a future colleague or boss.

Instead, in successfully addressing the employer's response to your counter-offer…

Use diplomatic, yet assertive phrases.

For example:
- *Is there any wiggle room?*
- *Is there a budget cap that I should be aware of?*

- *Do you mind if I ask you a question, if it's not too sensitive...What is the salary range and bonus targets for the role?*
- *I'm a bit disappointed. I expected an offer in the X to Y range, based on fair market value and my current compensation. What flexibility do you have?*
- *I'm extremely interested, but I must confess that I'm disappointed in the proposed bonus. Fair market value indicates 30 percent more for a position with this level of responsibility and 35 percent more for someone with my ability to contribute right away. How much room do you have?*
- *Is there an opportunity to structure the compensation so that I'm rewarded for meeting some short-term goals?*

It is amazing how much progress you can make in sweetening your offer when you ask graciously and diplomatically.

That said, the employer has **three potential responses** to your counter-offer, and your next step will depend on what they do.

1. What to do if the employer stands pat...

"I'm sorry, but that is all we've budgeted, and we consider it to be a very fair salary for the position."

Your response: don't give up yet! Perhaps you can negotiate a higher sign-on bonus or performance bonus that will bring the amount up to your reality or comfort level. Maybe the benefits are terrific or you can negotiate some additional perks.

Unless the number is totally out of the question, I recommend that you table the base salary discussion and move on continue negotiating other aspects of your compensation.

"OK, I understand your position. I do feel confident of my ability to achieve these goals for the company, so maybe we can look at enhancing the sign-on bonus or the performance bonus in a way that will make us both happy. Tell me more

about the bonuses and the benefit package. Is there any wiggle room there? Perhaps, I've overlooked something in my calculations."

2. What to do if they increase their offer a bit, but it's still below your expectations.

"Well, I guess we could go to 128,000, which is $3000 over our initial base salary offer."

What you should do: Follow the pattern of your initial response – that is be polite and enthusiastic, reiterate key challenges, and express your confidence in achieving results for the company.

"I appreciate your flexibility. I really do. But, you know, we talked about the employee relations issues you're having with your front-line employees in your divisional warehouses. I know that is affecting your productivity and I have a consistent history of getting great employee results in large, complex warehouse environments just like yours.

According to what you've shared with me, I've calculated that a 5 percent productivity boost would improve your bottom line by $3.5 million in the first year alone. Based on this kind of contribution, don't you agree that a salary in the $135,000 range is fair?"

Continue in this vein as long as the employer is receptive and you are able to document specific areas that where you can help the company and justify your value. It's always helpful to tie specific dollar benefits to your contributions, if you can. This will help the hiring authority see that hiring you will deliver more value than your cost to the company – or give them data that they can use to sell this to their higher ups for approval.

When you're satisfied that you've gone as far as you can go in negotiating base pay that is appropriate for your value and meets your expectations, agree to it enthusiastically. And then move on to phase two, where you negotiate the rest of the details of your total compensation package, including performance bonuses, benefits, and perks.

3. What to do if they accept your compensation counter-offer...

In this case, there's no need to negotiate your pay any further. You can then move on to discussing the rest of your total compensation package including benefits and perks.

> *"That sounds terrific. I appreciate your flexibility on the salary and bonus and I feel confident of my ability to deliver the results we've covered. Let's now discuss a couple of other items in the benefits area..."*

Special Side Note: About Sign-On Bonuses

If a company wants you badly enough but can't meet your base salary demands, they might try to sway you with a sign-on bonus. Signing bonuses are a one-time payment that isn't included in your base salary.

Typically they're offered to cover expenses you'll incur for changing employers such as relocation costs, cost-of-living differences or benefits you're leaving behind such as an upcoming bonus. They can also be offered in specific cases depending on the competitive job market for a specific HR competency.

A sign-on bonus is really a good-faith demonstration that the employer agrees you're worth more than your annual compensation and it's a way of "bribing" you to come to work for them – without increasing their annual compensation costs or creating internal pay equity issues with your future colleagues.

That said, here are a few mild warnings:
- With sign-on bonuses, typically you have to sign a contract committing to a period of time on the job and, if you don't stay for that length of time, you have to pay the bonus back!

- Quite often, signing or hiring bonuses can be taxed at a higher rate, as high as 41.5 percent. Ouch!
- When you negotiate for a sign-on bonus, you are getting a ONE time bonus. You'll always benefit more by getting those same dollars in your salary, as they will have created value year after year.

The best way to think about what your sign-on bonus should be is to methodically assess the expenses you'll incur for changing employers -- such as relocation, cost-of-living differences, differences in your current versus your new base salary, how challenging the new position will be and the value of other competing job offers you may be weighing.

Strategy #7:
Once You've Agreed On The Cash Comp Items, Then Move On To Negotiating The "Non-Cash" Elements on Your Wish List (Bennies & Perks)

"Bennies" is slang for benefits, "perks" for hiring perquisites. They are important for two reasons. First, they can complement a solid salary, making the total package even better. Second, if the salary you've been offered isn't quite what you expected, adding on some of these non-cash, often-nontaxable extras can bring the entire offer very close to the figure you had in mind.

Candidly, most companies offer fixed benefit plans that are the same for every employee – and as such don't (or prefer not to) haggle over them.

But **unless you ask, you will never know if an item is negotiable or not.** Here are some examples of requests you might make in this area:

I realize you don't have as much flexibility as I'd like on the starting salary, but I'm wondering if you'd consider an extra week's vacation. It's personally significant to me and would enable me to visit my family on the other side of the country.

Because I have full coverage through my spouse, I won't need to take advantage of your health insurance benefit. Is there a chance this could be swapped for a cash benefit?

I've just begun my Masters in Human Resources and I'm excited about the added expertise I'll be able to offer you as a result. My current company covers the tuition and the two days per month of class time. Is that something you could continue here?

The point: Despite your best efforts, if the starting salary is still a bit lower than you wanted, concentrate on squeezing into your offer some "non-cash" benefits and perks. These include items such as extra vacation time, extra time off (paid or unpaid), subsidized daycare or flexible hours and the like.

Although extra time off or a flexible schedule won't make up for getting cold hard cash in hand, such benefits can increase your job satisfaction and give you a positive feeling about the company.

If you could negotiate an extra week of vacation, how much would that be worth to you in dollars? Probably more than the pay for working a typical 40-60 hour HR work week, right?

If you have other commitments in your life that require some flexibility, negotiating the option of working from home into your compensation package is of greater value than a one-time check could ever be. (It's the bonus that keeps on giving!)

Again, refer to the list on pages 133-134 of potential cash and non-cash benefits and perks to prioritize those that will make a significant difference to you.

Strategy #8:
Don't Go Back To The Well
More Than Twice

When a company makes you an offer, don't go back to the well more than twice. Anything beyond that is going to frustrate the hell out of them.

For example, let's say after your first counter-offer, they said they'd get back to you. The person with whom you are negotiating may wait a day or two before contacting you again to enable them to consult with higher ups (or just to "make you sweat"). Don't worry. If you were professional and not unreasonable, you're fine.

When they finally contact you, if they've revised their offer and met your expectations, then thank them and accept the offer.

However, if they are close but still short of what you want, **recognize that if you want them to sweeten their offer more, then this is your second and final "trip to the well."** If it's worth it to you, then say:

"Jennifer, thank you. We are close. Everything is great except for one point. Is there any wiggle room at all here?"

"Jack, everything looks fantastic, except for two minor details. Is there any way at all these two items can be accommodated?"

"Barbara, thanks for all your help with this. I'm thrilled you were able to deliver X, Y and Z. On point A, however I was still hoping for B. Is there any flexibility here at all?"

After these are discussed and addressed, DON'T negotiate further. That was your second and final trip to the well. I have heard more than one angry HR hiring executive comment:

"Does she want the damn job or not? If she asks for one more freakin' thing we are moving on."

When you have been to the well twice, now it is time to get off the pot and make a decision. So, if they say:

"I'm sorry. This is really the best we can do…"

Then you conclude with:

"Thanks so much again for going to bat for me. This is something that I really want to do and I need to review everything one last time. May I get back with you first thing tomorrow morning with my final decision? This is a big career step for me and I just want to sleep on it overnight."

Or you can simply not wait and accept it on the spot!

The key: Don't be greedy! One sure way to lose everything you have achieved through your negotiating efforts is to go overboard. There comes a point in every negotiation when you have obtained everything that you could reasonably have hoped to achieve. At that point you should thank the person you are dealing with and accept the position.

If you don't know when to stop negotiating, you run the risk of having the company decide that it made a mistake by offering you the job in the first place. Most organizations will want to treat you fairly and make you happy, but few want to hire a prima donna. Being perceived as greedy or unreasonable may cause the offer to be withdrawn. Even if it does not, you will have done immeasurable harm to your career with that employer.

Strategy #9:
Keep Your Recruiters In The Loop

If you have a headhunter who is going to be paid for your successful placement, keep her in the negotiation loop. Some will want to negotiate directly with the employer on your behalf as many may have a personal, long-standing relationship with the employer that you can take advantage of.

On the other hand, if their negotiations don't seem to be going well, you need to determine whether the recruiter truly understands the limitations of her employer client or if she simply just does not want to raise tough issues. In those cases, you may need to take regain control of directly negotiating with your potential employer.

At the very least, if you decide to do all the negotiating yourself, engage your recruiter as a sounding board. Top recruiters will guide you through each of the items that you seek – and most provide excellent counsel and advice.

Strategy #10:
Get the Details Of The Revised Offer in Writing And Review It Again

If you have re-negotiated any changes to the original written offer, ask for a revised offer letter. Again, always, always get everything in writing. If the employer promises a salary review at three months, get it in writing. If they promise you an extra week of vacation in your first year, get it in writing. If they say, "Sure, we'll increase that 401(k) contribution for the company by January, instead of next year," get it in writing.

Words, sadly, mean nothing. They are easily forgotten and leave you with no recourse. You may also want to consider having any detailed employment agreements reviewed by an attorney.

Strategy #11:
Accept The Offer Enthusiastically!

When you are ready to accept, sign your offer letter. Then scan and e-mail or mail it back to your new employer. Always call upon acceptance and thank them for the opportunity. Let them know how excited you are to get started. If you need to adjust your start date or need to keep it open, then just tell them.

Some employers only start new hires on certain days to minimize their orientation expenses. If anything should delay your anticipated start date, be sure to call right away. If your start date is longer than two weeks out, you should call weekly to let them know you are still on track for your start date.

On the other hand, if you do get to the point where you are going to reject an offer, do so with the utmost professionalism. You never know where the future leads and it is never good to burn a bridge behind you. Thank them for the offer and tell them that you have decided to pursue another opportunity. If they ask for details you can offer them up if you'd like, but in most cases, it is best to keep your reasons general in nature.

Strategy #12
Don't Entertain Counter-Offers From Your Current Employer

I'll put it as simply and as plainly as possible: Don't entertain counteroffers from your current company. If you have progressed all the way to the offer stage with the new employer, you should also, by that time, be committed to leaving your current firm.

Just think back to why you started looking in the first place. Whatever your original reasons for deciding to leave your present employer may have been, those reasons are still valid, no matter how much money they promise you to entice you to stay.

You may have outgrown your boss or your job. You may find you need to work in a company with a better future. Perhaps you want a more collegial or HR-friendly environment. You don't really expect those burning issues to go away just because your original employer has fattened your paycheck, do you?

If you're still not convinced, here's the clincher: Even if your current employer has found a way to entice you to stay a little while longer, in your boss's mind you're already gone. Even though you may be bringing home a larger salary, you may discover that you're no longer factored into long-term plans. After all, who knows when you might consider leaving again? So there's no real bargain to be had by accepting your current company's counteroffer, no matter how sincerely they say they want you to stay.

Finally, accepting your current company's counteroffer is also unfair to the hiring company and the recruiter. If you've interviewed with them to the extent that they're ready to extend an offer, they've already spent many hours on you, interviewing, getting you through the process, checking references, and so forth. In the meantime, they've also passed up other great candidates for you. By accepting the counteroffer, you will have put everyone (including yourself) in a terrible position. So that should be avoided at all costs.

Summary

You have the most leverage in the interview once an offer has been made. Make sure you give yourself time to understand the total pay package you're being offered first before you start negotiating. Once you're received your offer in writing, then prepare your negotiating strategy, prioritize your "wish list" and don't be impatient with the give and take.

Be professional, remind the person you're negotiating with of the value you bring to the company and how excited you are to join the team – and you've set the stage for maximizing your job offer and total pay package.

14

THE FINAL STEP:
HOW TO LEAVE YOUR OLD JOB
GRACEFULLY – JUST IN CASE YOU
EVER WANT (OR NEED) TO GO BACK

You've reached the end of the road! You've just accepted a new HR position. My hat's off to you.

More money. Better title. More exciting responsibilities.

Way to go!

I know you're excited. You probably feel as if you could fly. But before you get too full of yourself, here's my advice...

Stop! There's one final step if you're currently employed. You want to carefully plan your exit from your current organization – so you don't burn any bridges. No matter how you feel about your current job and your boss now, you may want (or need) to return to that organization again...or you may cross paths in the future with some of those you've left behind.

The Story of Eileen Raymond

No one illustrates the importance of not burning bridges better than Eileen.

Her journey was highlighted recently in *HR Executive.* As described in one of their featured articles, she was the global director of talent acquisition for KPMG, based in New York.

She left that firm to join BearingPoint, its spun-off consulting organization as director of recruiting.

However, after giving birth to her second child, she heard from a former HR colleague who asked if she would consider coming back to KPMG.

She was initially reluctant because she felt her status as a new mom would prevent her from meeting the rugged demands of the job.

However, she relented and decided to accept the interview anyway and discovered that KPMG had changed dramatically since she had been there years earlier.

Its support for flexible work arrangements -- including the option of working from home -- was very appealing to her and had been featured in *Working Mother* magazine along with other positive workplace changes.

So, she rejoined the company in HR, as executive director in charge of recruiting experienced candidates. When she returned, she was thrilled and...

She helped facilitate the return of other former KPMG employees, just like her -- including 10 other recruiters!

That's right, she's brought back other former KPMG human resources alums just like herself. And as many as 15% of KPMG's experienced-new-hires are actually "boomerangs."

Her story illustrates an important workplace change.

"Boomeranging" -- that is the practice of returning to your old organization as a rehire -- is happening with greater frequency. It used to be leaving a job in HR was the kiss of death. You were regarded as disloyal and undesirable. See ya later. Don't let the door hit your butt on the way out. You know the drill.

However, plenty of enlightened organizations are reaching out to rehire their former HR employees. Finding great HR people is not easy. Employers increasingly recognize that talented people in HR have a natural desire to explore and further their careers -- and that the act of leaving shouldn't be viewed as giving the organization the middle finger and committing an unforgivable sin.

If you want to keep this important career avenue available for you, it's crucial that you know how to properly leave your organization, while keeping your reputation intact. To that end, here's a step-by-step plan doing exactly that so that you've set the stage for your potential return, if necessary:

Step 1: Carefully plan your transition first.

Don't quit your current job until everything about your new job is negotiated and confirmed. Signed offer letter or employment contract? Check. Benefits package? Check. Start date? Check. You get the idea.

Draft a transition plan for your responsibilities and any unfinished projects. Don't leave your boss buried in your unfinished work. Create a list with your recommendations on how your work can be shifted to others in the department until your position is filled.

Determine your "story." Think through how you will explain the reason for your departure to your manager and coworkers. Whatever explanation you provide, keep your story consistent and the reasons positive.

Step 2: Write your resignation letter.

Resist the urge to go negative. No matter how pissed off you may be with the organization, don't write anything rude, derogatory, or mean. You may need to be in contact with your boss later (you may even end up working with him or her again) so it is better to be respectful in your letter. Otherwise, your overly emotional, ugly words may come back to haunt you. Here's an extreme example of what not to write: _"Susan, I quit. I hated working here. You were the worst HR boss I ever had and I'm_ *thrilled to be leaving. You also owe me $7,000 in unused vacation that you never let me take. You suck. -Brian."*

Instead, think of your resignation letter as a brief thank you note. It should express your gratitude for having had the opportunity to work in the organization and with your boss, and include the date of your last day on the job. It should read something like this:

> *Dear Sarah,*
> *It has been my honor to work for the ABC Company. This letter is to notify you that I will be leaving to accept a new position with another company as of [a date which is AT LEAST two weeks from the date of your conversation and letter]. Please accept my thanks for our association, and best regards to you and the entire company for the future.*
> *Sincerely,*
> *George Smith*

Highlight your achievements. Don't boast, but in your letter feel free to mention a few of the projects you worked on and how proud you are of them. This is important because your letter of resignation may be archived, along with any negative remarks the higher-ups may add to your file. Putting your achievements down are a plus if you ever apply to be rehired, as your file will be accessed and your accomplishments will be one of the first things noted.

Step 3: Tell your manager before anyone else.

Refrain from saying anything to your colleagues until you've met with your boss. No matter what, you owe your manager the courtesy of informing him or her first.

Quit in person and bring your resignation letter with you. It's always best and most respectful if you resign in person and can provide closure. But if your boss works in a different geographic location, make a telephone appointment and then follow up with a brief email, attaching your resignation letter.

Don't beat around the bush or try and cushion the blow. Be prepared, direct, and polite. Most busy managers will appreciate a no-bull approach. Verbally, you might say something like:

> *"I've been considering my options here for some time, and I've decided it's time for me to move on. I am grateful for the opportunities I've found here, but I must give my two weeks' notice."*

> *OR... "I need to let you know that I have been offered a new position at another company. I have really enjoyed working here, but I need to give you my two weeks' notice as of today. Does it work for you if my last day is [whatever two weeks from then is]?"*

Give adequate notice. Providing a two-week notice is the global norm. Fewer than two weeks and your employer risks not having an adequate replacement in place. More than three weeks and your employer will be wondering why you're still around. Be aware that some bosses won't take kindly to you being "the decider." However, if your job is complex and will be difficult to fill or if you are in a senior-level HR position, be prepared to provide additional time for your employer to find your replacement and offer to train the person.

Be prepared to discuss your reasons for leaving. Chances are you've been working with this boss for some time, and whatever your reasons are for leaving, he or she may have some questions. Prepare a response that is concise and understandable. If you are quitting because you hate your job, try to frame your answers in an inoffensive way. Instead of "I hate working here" you might say *"I think its time that I head in a different direction with my career."*

Step 4: Prepare for the unexpected.

Be ready to leave your job that day. Sometimes managers take it personally that you've resigned and will inform you that giving them notice is unnecessary because you'll be leaving immediately! Know beforehand if this is your firm's standard practice or assess if your boss is likely to respond in this way. But, you may not be able to accurately predict this, so be ready.

Prepare for a counteroffer. Your boss may value you much more than you think and make a counteroffer to stay. Being polite, professional and dignified about your resignation could make this possible. You will need to consider in advance whether a pay raise, a promotion, or other incentives is enough to change your mind. **Let me again be clear: for the reasons mentioned in the previous chapter, I'm biased -- I don't think you should consider ANY counter-offer!** But, it's your decision not mine – and if you do decide to accept their counter, protect yourself by getting it in writing and signed by your boss and his supervisor.

Be ready if the boss asks you if he or she had anything to do with your decision. If they were a factor, be truthful without being punitive or cruel: *"It was a factor, but not the entire reason. I felt our working styles and approaches never meshed as well as I truly wished they had. Still, the overall experience here has been positive; and with this opportunity, I feel excited to have new challenges."*

Step 5: Reach agreement with your boss on how others will be told.

Let the boss be the decision-maker on this. Your boss may send out a company-wide email, or he/she may ask you to send out your own personal notice. However, don't go blabbing about your departure all over the organization before you have discussed these details with your boss.

Give your boss time to absorb and process the information. If your boss is slow to respond with an announcement about your departure, it could be that an attractive counter-offer is being considered and it will be awkward if you have already announced your plans to coworkers. If that's not the case, to speed things up, suggest to the boss that you tell coworkers individually and volunteer to write a short email that your boss can then distribute within the department.

Step 6: Give notice to everyone else affected by your departure.

Once the word is out, be sure to personally tell other managers, clients or key employees with whom you have worked that you have resigned. Say it in a way that "thanks" the person for helping you develop your career. For example:

> _"I don't know if you've heard, but I am resigning to take a position at another company. Before I leave I wanted to be sure to let you know how much I've enjoyed working with you."_

Here's the deal: These people may someday leave for other jobs too and you want them to have positive memories of you. Who knows when they can impact your next career change.

Meet individually with your mentors and sponsors within the company. Beyond your own department, if you have mentors or anyone within the company who has acted as your sponsor, quickly schedule time to let them know you're leaving and why.

Tie up any work-related loose ends. This is both a respectful and considerate thing to do and your boss and your coworkers are sure to appreciate it. Consider creating a file that explains where you left off on any long-running projects, and other essentials your replacement might need to know about things you worked on. Make sure all of your files are in order, labeled, and easily located -- you don't want to have frantic coworkers calling you after you have left the company because they can't find one of your key projects. This is especially important if you are working on a cross-functional team or if you're in the middle of a crucial new HR initiative. Once you have given your notice, discuss with your team which people will take on which duties or until a replacement is found for you.

Step 7: Prepare your exit and transition.

Be prepared to tell your story in an exit interview. Don't sidestep this just because you're in HR yourself. On any questionnaire or face-to-face exit discussion, stay consistent with your "story" and what you've already told your boss in your resignation meeting. There should be no surprises when he or she receives the exit interview feedback report.

Don't be stunned if you're escorted out by security. If your new employer happens to be a direct competitor of the company (example: you're a Coke employee joining PepsiCo), you may be asked to leave immediately upon your resignation. Many companies will assign security personnel to watch you while you clean out your cube, office or workspace and then lead you out.

Work as hard as you can, all the way up until the final minute on your last day. The best way to ensure you leave on a positive note is to work hard to ensuring a smooth transition right up until the time you're walking out the door.

Step 8: Capture your contacts and stay in touch.

Plan to maintain contact with everyone you've worked with. To facilitate this, add your former boss, colleagues and clients to your LinkedIn network (including their e-mail contact information)...and while you're at it update your LinkedIn profile and your resume too.

Summary

The goal of resigning gracefully is to always strategically position yourself constructively with the people you forged a relationship with while at work – and enable you to positive leverage these relationships in the future.

In addition, by following these eight steps, you've set the stage for good references and you've left the door open to potentially be rehired down the road – if need be.

15

Extra Bonus Chapter:
HOW TO CRUSH PHONE INTERVIEWS
& VIDEO INTERVIEWS

This book focuses primarily on the **in-person, face to face interview** because it is the most common and popular form of interviewing...and where the important hiring decisions will be made. However, there are two other interviews you should be prepared for as well and they are:

1. The phone interview
2. The video interview

In this special bonus chapter, we'll look at each one, starting with...

Phone Interviews

The phone interview is typically the first contact you'll have with an organization...and its <u>primary</u> purpose is to screen you out of the selection process.

Make no mistake about it. The person on the other end of the line wants to cull a long list of candidates quickly and cheaply. To them, it's just like setting up a date though an online dating service. If they like your profile, the safest thing for them to do is meet for coffee first to see if you are normal and not crazy as hell. Dinner would be too much of a commitment. In their minds, the phone interview follows the same logic. It is the coffee date and the face-to-face interview is dinner.

Also, over the phone, fast judgments are being made about you. And if you don't make the cut, you're out of the running and you won't get a second chance. In this way, phone interviews have all of the critical, "make-or-break" qualities of a face-to-face interview with none of the advantages.

Finally, because you can't see the interviewer's face, you have no idea if they're smiling, nodding, or frowning at something you're saying. It's like operating in the dark with no visual cues to help you interpret how the conversation is going.

Nervous yet? Don't be.

Here Are Strategies For Crushing Your Next Phone Interview:

#1: Schedule the interview at your convenience.

If you get an unexpected cold call from a company or recruiter, requesting a few minutes of your time, *defer the conversation.* Don't get sucked into answering any questions on the spot. Instead, express appreciation for the call, and ask to schedule the interview at a mutually acceptable date and time. Even if it's later in the same day, rescheduling gives you time to prepare, do some quick research on the company and collect your thoughts.

Most of the time, hiring managers are pretty flexible when it comes to scheduling a phone conversation. Assuming you get the choice, always schedule your interview for the time of day you are most alert and on your game. Personally, I would never, ever schedule a phone interview first thing in the morning. I need a little while to warm up first. On the other hand, I have a friend who is at her best at the crack of dawn. So for her, the earlier the better.

Make sure you allow enough time away from your other commitments for the call. A rule of thumb is to allow an hour, though most phone interviews will take a lot less time than that.

#2: Prepare for the phone interview the same way you would an in-person job interview. Do all your pre-interview research, know the company, review the job description, list out the questions you want to ask, and even write down some key points you want to make. The more you can do, the more prepared you will be and the more confident you will feel.

#3: Use a land line instead of a mobile phone. However, if you absolutely must take the call from your cell phone, make sure you are in an area that has good reception and you're in a quiet environment. Do whatever you can to ensure quiet, uninterrupted time. This call is too important to risk dropping it, interference, sun spots, aliens…whatever. It destroys momentum and it is distracting.

Sound quality is more reliable on a land line which is why it's preferred. If this is not possible, then check your mobile reception from the location you'll be taking the call perhaps by taking a test call from a friend.

#4: Take the call at your home or the quietest spot you can find. Public places like restaurants and coffee houses are too noisy and unpredictable. Even if you could find yourself a nice quiet spot in a park, you'd still have to deal with nature. Birds can be surprisingly loud. Don't interview at your current office, because that's too risky. And never, ever, interview and drive. Safety first.

#5: Take that call standing up rather than sitting down. You've heard the phrase, "think on your feet." It is a physiological fact. Your circulation will be better, which will feed your brain and cause your lungs to operate at full capacity. All of this will make your voice project more confidently.

#6: Lay out your phone interview materials. One benefit of having a phone interview is that you can have all your materials in front of you for handy reference. Have a pen and pad for jotting down notes. If possible skip the computer for note taking, as it can easily become a distraction. Remember, you want to stay 100% focused on your conversation.

Also have a glass of water within reach, a copy of your resume (in case they want you to "walk through it") and information about the company. Some people like to have the company's website in front of them on a computer screen and others like to have a copy of their resume or job description.

Create and print out a cheat sheet for yourself using the notes you've jotted down based on tips from this book. One of the big advantages of a phone interview is that it can work like an open book test.

#7: Give the interviewer what they're looking for.

What are hiring managers and HR people looking for when they call you for a phone interview? Two things:

First, they're looking for your responses to questions like:

"Why are you interested in this opportunity?"
"Tell me about your HR experience with the XYZ Company?"
"Why are you leaving (or have left) your current job?"

You should recognize these kinds of general questions, because we covered them in Chapter 5. In fact, reviewing this particular chapter is great prep...especially if you have thorny work history issues like employment gaps or if you've been recently fired. These particular elements of your resume will definitely catch their attention and will be probed in depth. By the way, if you were terminated from your last job, tell them the truth...but remember, *how you tell them* is the important point. Again, use the information in Chapter 5 to help you here.

Secondly the interviewer is trying to determine if you're a potential fit for the position. To help them here, you should ask as early as you can: *"What does your ideal candidate look like?"* It's a valuable question to ask because it might be a little different than what's listed in the job description. It's their "ideal" candidate, after all. Once you know that, you have a blueprint of what specific aspects of your HR background you should emphasize most over the phone to position yourself as a top candidate.

#8: Dress in a killer outfit – even though it's only a phone interview. While it is tempting to dress down for a phone interview, do yourself a favor and play the part. The clothes we put on have a major impact on how we behave. I have a close friend who's noticed that the days she wears her red designer Gucci pumps, she's got a little more strut in her step than if she's kicking around in her yoga pants and sneakers. Take a look around one day and see how many people shuffle around when they wear gym shoes or flip flops. You'd think this stuff doesn't matter, but it really does.

The idea is, if you want to make sure you behave and sound like a professional, you should dress like a professional. It will put you in the right frame of mind and help you focus. Put on your best suit jacket if that makes you feel fantastic. And it doesn't even matter if it's the same one you'll wear to the face-to face interview – they can't see it, after all.

#9: Don't fill in the gaps. Be prepared for pauses and silence. Sometimes this can make even the most experienced HR candidates uncomfortable and can lead you to blurt out unnecessary statements. Remember that during phone interviews, the interviewer needs to take notes, and when they don't speak immediately, they are probably just busy writing.

#10: Project a confident voice. When you are on the call, you need to keep the interviewer's attention and not allow them to be distracted. So keep your answers short. Be sure to modulate your voice (no monotone), and insert questions into the conversation.

You also want to make ensure that your voice is clear and doesn't go dry. Keep your voice and mouth unobstructed. No gum, food or resting your chin on your hand. Consider consuming a throat lozenge with menthol an hour before the interview. This will cause you to breathe easier, reduce your risk of coughing and smooth your voice.

#11: Know the salary range for the position. If you are asked your current salary or your compensation expectations, use the strategies discussed earlier in Chapter 5. However, if the compensation for the position is not brought up by the interviewer, ask about the compensation package or the "salary range" for the position. This may be contrary to what others may advise you to do. However, I believe life's too short. Don't waste your time on HR positions that don't meet (or are at least near) your compensation expectations.

#12: Finalize the next steps. At the end of the interview, you can get an inkling of what they think about you by asking what the next steps are. Try suggesting a few days when you can come in for an interview. Their answer may give you hints.

#13: Close at the end of the interview. Here's how: *"Janet, I really appreciate your time today. I'm genuinely interested in this opportunity."* Let them end the phone call and the conversation first. Following this simple yet gracious social gesture leaves the other party with a subtly biased good feeling toward you.

#14: After the phone interview concludes, immediately fire off a quick e-mail or text to your interviewer to thank them for his or her time. This goes a long way in indicating that you are interested in the position.

To sum up, phone interviews, just like in-person face-to-face interviews, require careful planning and preparation.

Video Interviews

Due to cost, efficiency and ever-evolving technology, video interviewing is extremely popular and efficient. It gives employers the benefit of not having to fly you in for interviews.

In some organizations, a video interview has all the impact and decision-making influence of a face-to face interview. Therefore, everything you have read in this book applies to video interviewing as well.

Whatever video technology is used, treat this interview like any other. That is, be thoroughly researched, rehearsed, and ready to solve and serve!

Here Are Some Key Strategies For Nailing Video Interviews:

#1: Practice using the technology. Technology is changing all the time. As we speak, many video interviews are done using Skype, FaceTime or a similar service. However, no matter what technology the employer is using, you don't want the flow of your interview interrupted – so make sure you have the software installed (or the technology readily available) – and practice using it. Skype for example, gives you the option to see yourself in a small window as you are on camera. Test this option out in advance and determine whether it is helpful or distracting.

#2: Dress in professional interview attire, just as you would for an in-person interview. It also goes without saying that you should make sure the outfit is updated and professional. However, like newscasters, you can get away with wearing shorts or jeans, since only the top part of your body will be visible -- but I don't recommend it. If you make the mistake of only dressing from the waist up and leaving your PJs on for the bottom half, you never know what might make you unexpectedly stand up. Don't risk the embarrassment! (For more tips on interviewing attire, see Chapter 1).

#3: Set the video camera at eye level. If you're using your laptop camera, don't make the mistake of staring down at it. This will make it appear as if you are looming over the interviewer…and you'll come across as more intense and domineering. So prop the laptop up on books until the camera is eye height so that the conversation feels more natural.

#4: Maintain eye contact with the camera and speak directly into the lens. When you look away, it becomes noticeable, and you may appear unfocused and shifty. Also, when you're not talking, keep looking at the lens, as you are still "on camera." Practice giving your answers to the camera and train your eye not to drop. Even though you won't see the interviewer, it will appear like you are looking right at them.

#5: Put a light on the other side of the camera. Lighting is very important. Not only should the room be well lit, but you should put a big lamp on the other side of the camera facing you so that you are fully lit from the front. This will make sure that you don't look dark and brooding on camera. NOTE: Test run your lighting with someone before your interview to make sure it doesn't look like there is a spotlight on you. You should be well lit, but not glowing in the dark!

#6: Choose a neutral, uncluttered background. No matter how good you look, if your background looks bad, it will reflect poorly on you. Position yourself a few feet from a wall, and have a few tasteful decor components in the background (e.g. a painting, a plant, or an organized bookshelf). Imagine meeting with the CEO of a huge company, and think about how their desk is positioned and try to create the same setup. A white wall absolutely works, but if you have the time to "design" your set, it will certainly boost the impression you make!

#7: Use reminders. Place reminder signs behind the camera, such as "Smile," "Eye contact," "Speak slowly," and so on. Being on camera may make you tense, so remember to smile.

#8: Watch extraneous sounds. Be aware that your microphone may be sensitive and will pick up small background noises, such as a tapping a pen, sniffling, or people/pets in the next room.

#9: Sit on a hard chair or stool. You don't want to be too comfortable and slouchy. Choose a chair that makes you sit up straight. It's that simple.

#10: Notify the interviewer immediately if you are experiencing any technical problems. This could include such difficulties as hearing the question or an excessive delay in the sound or picture. Recognize that there will be a slight delay as data is compressed and transmitted. This can be to your advantage because you'll have a few more milliseconds to think of your responses.

If there's more than one interviewer…write down the names of the interviewers, and use those names when appropriate so that it's clear to whom you are directing a question or comment.

#11: Have a glass of water in arm's reach. An unexpected cough, dry mouth, or nerves can happen at any time. So, keep that glass of water handy in the even you suddenly need it.

#12: Know where your mute button is! No matter how much you prepare, things can go wrong and you may need to hit "mute" unexpectedly. Figure out where it is in advance so you can quickly turn sound off and step out of the video shot if necessary.

To sum up, more and more employers are doing video interviews to speed up the hiring process. Follow these tips and those in the rest of this book and you could be in your new HR job sooner than you expect.

And finally, if you are given the choice or if you can arrange it, try to interview <u>in-person</u> rather than by video or by phone. Nothing replaces in-person face time.

16

FINAL THOUGHTS

The goal of this book was to provide you with more than just an interviewing how-to guide. It was also intended to provide strategies for marketing yourself and your brand that will help you for the rest of your HR career.

That said, here are a few closing thoughts:

Your ability to interview well is an irreplaceable skill. One of the most valuable commodities on the planet is the ability to sell yourself, stand out from your competition and position your accomplishments compellingly in an interview setting.

Even the most experienced and savvy HR professionals are jittery when they face interviews. Clearly some nervousness is natural. However, if you internalize the insights in this book, you should be more than prepared to transform this anxiety into excitement, energy, enthusiasm – and job offers!

For these reasons, keep this book close and your interviewing skills polished. In today's uncertain and volatile job market, you'll never know when you'll be faced with interviewing out of necessity -- or because a phenomenal HR opportunity has suddenly arrived at your doorstop.

And when this happens, the tactics and strategies in this book will equip you to capitalize on these opportunities and transform them into exciting new avenues that will advance your career in Human Resources.

I wish you much success.

Onward!

Alan Collins

Alan Collins

P.S. If you're interested in more strategies and tactics for career success in Human Resources, please feel free to connect with us online:

Follow us on Twitter:
@SuccessInHR

Subscribe to our Newsletter:
SuccessInHR.com

Connect with us on LinkedIn:
http://LinkedIn.com/SuccessInHR

THE BRYAN A. COLLINS SCHOLARSHIP PROGRAM

The Bryan A. Collins Memorial Scholarship Program awards scholarship grants every year to minority students who demonstrate excellence in pursuit of their college degrees. Students selected for this scholarship must embody the values embraced by the late Bryan A. Collins -- great with people, great at academics and great in extra-curricular leadership activities.

Bryan Collins was a rising star and well-respected student leader at Tennessee State University. Bryan received his B.S. degree in Biology from TSU in May 2005. At the time of his passing, he was enrolled in the Masters program in physical therapy and anxiously looking forward to commencing his doctoral studies. On campus, he was a leader in the Kappa Alpha Psi fraternity, served on the Civic Committee, the Community Service Committee and help set strategic direction as a Board Member of the fraternity.

In addition, he found much success outside the classroom. He was voted Mr. Tennessee State first runner-up, was involved in the Student Union Board of Governors, was a founding member of the Generation of Educated Men and worked closely with the Tennessee State University dean of admissions and records.

Bryan found comfort and relaxation in sports, music, movies, video games, friends, good parties and just spending time with his family relaxing at home.

Key contributors to Bryan's scholarship program include the PepsiCo Foundation, the Motorola Foundation, Pamela Hewitt & Warren Lawson of Chicago and many other organizations and individuals. Additional details about Bryan, the scholarship program and how to contribute can be found at the scholarship website at: www.BryanCollinsScholarship.org.

ABOUT THE AUTHOR

Alan Collins is **Founder of Success in HR**, a company dedicated to empowering HR professionals and executives around the globe with insights and tools for enhancing their careers.

He currently serves 14,000+ HR subscribers through his flagship newsletter, "Success in HR" (www.SuccessInHR.com) and inspires countless others through his books, presentations and coaching.

Alan was formerly Vice President of Human Resources at PepsiCo where he led HR initiatives for their North American Quaker Oats, Gatorade and Tropicana businesses. With 25 years as an HR executive and professional, Alan's corporate and operating human resources experience is extensive. He led an organization of 60 HR directors, managers and professionals spread across 21 different locations in North America, where he was accountable for their performance, careers and success. He and his team provided HR strategic and executional oversight for a workforce of over 7000 employees supporting $8 billion in sales. Alan also served as the HR M&A lead in integrating new acquisitions as well as divesting existing businesses; and he provided HR leadership for one of the largest change initiatives in the history of the PepsiCo organization.

Alan is author of the *Unwritten HR Rules* and *HR Resume Secrets.* Both have been consistently ranked among Amazon's best selling books for HR professionals. In addition, he has written over 100 articles and special reports on HR that have appeared in *HR Executive Magazine, HRM Today* and other nationally-known publications for human resources professionals. He has also taught at various Chicago-area universities.

He received his B.S. degree in Management and M.S. in Industrial Relations & Human Resources from Purdue. More about Alan and his works can be accessed at: www.SuccessInHR.com.

Made in the USA
Lexington, KY
30 July 2019